2000

D0821003

John Fante
His Novels and Novellas

Twayne's United States Authors Series

Joseph M. Flora, Editor

University of North Carolina, Chapel Hill

TUSAS 717

JOHN FANTE IN ROSEVILLE, CALIFORNIA, 1937
By permission of Joyce Fante.

John Fante
His Novels and Novellas

Catherine J. Kordich

University of California, Santa Cruz

Twayne Publishers
New York

ASHEVILLE-BUNCOMBE LIBRARY SYSTEM

Twayne's United States Authors Series No. 717

John Fante: His Novels and Novellas
Catherine J. Kordich

Copyright © 2000 by Twayne Publishers

All rights reserved. No part of this book may be reproduced or transmitted in any
form or by any means, electronic or mechanical, including photocopying, recording, or
by any information storage and retrieval system, without permission in writing from
the Publisher.

Twayne Publishers
1633 Broadway
New York, NY 10019

Library of Congress Cataloging-in-Publication Data
Kordich, Catherine J.
    John Fante : his novels and novellas / Catherine J. Kordich
        p. cm. --(Twayne's United States authors series ; TUSAS 717)
    Includes bibliographical references (p.) and index.
    ISBN 0-8057-1613-0 (alk. paper)
        1. Fante, John, 1909---Criticism and interpretation. 2. Italian Americans in literature.
    I. Title.   II. Series
    PS3511.A594 Z75 2000
    813'.52--dc21

This paper meets the requirements of ANSI/NISO Z3948-1992 (Permanence of
Paper).

10 9 8 7 6 5 4 3 2 1

Printed in the United States of America

ASHEVILLE-BUNCOMBE LIBRARY SYSTEM

Dedicated to my grandparents,
John and Margaret Glenn, Lavonne Solie, and Joy Woodfin

Contents

Preface

Though John Fante published novels, short stories, and screenplays for almost 50 years, his literary accomplishments were largely ignored until the end of his life, when fortuitous events led to Black Sparrow Press's involvement in Fante's works. Swift acclaim followed their 1980 republication of his novel *Ask the Dust*. Since Fante's 1983 death, subsequent republications and the release of new material (including those manuscripts found posthumously) converted readers in increasing number. Enthusiastic reviews and word-of-mouth buzz transformed Fante's longtime underground fame into mainstream literary readership. Translations of Fante's novels gained him international celebrity, particularly in France and Germany. Though Fante died only three years into the surge of interest in his work, at the end he knew that his works had finally reached an appreciative audience.

John Fante was born and raised in Boulder, Colorado, the eldest of four children in a very poor household. As a young man, at the height of the depression, Fante made his way to Los Angeles, California. Fante's ethnic identity—a second-generation Italian American—was at perpetual odds with the Anglo mainstream culture that he lived within, and often sought out, for the majority of his life. Fante's fascination with identity is clearly evident in his works of fiction: all of his protagonists cope with the ethnic and social conflicts Fante himself negotiated.

During his lifetime, Fante's work was frequently compared to William Saroyan's (both wrote of ethnic outsiders, both were gifted humorists). Fante studied, and sought to emulate, H. L. Mencken's clear and dynamic prose. Fante was most influenced by the writers he mentions in his novels: Norwegian author Knut Hamsun, Sinclair Lewis, Fyodor Mikhailovich Dostoyevsky, and Gustave Flaubert. Fante responded strongly to these authors, whose characters reckon with interior schisms among instinct, duty, and desire. From these authors Fante learned the use of the revealing detail; his own novels link material elements of setting to serious symbolic purpose. Fante also admired Sherwood Anderson, and Anderson's influence is apparent in Fante's succinctly sketched characters. Fante deviates from the high realism of some of his literary heroes, particularly Flaubert, in his poetic and emotional lyricism. This lyrical quality of Fante's prose is today often considered anticipatory of the Beats, and the poetic stream-of-consciousness musings of Fante's protagonists support this comparison. This is among the first generation of book-length studies of John Fante's novels and novellas and is certainly a product of the remarkable latter-day interest in Fante's work. Fante's short stories, of which there are many, are only discussed here when they are directly relevant to the discussion of the longer works.[1]

Chapter 1 gives an overview of Fante's life and locates topical and stylistic emphases in his literary output. It includes brief discussions of Fante's circumstances and times in order to contextualize his writings.

Set in Colorado, Fante's first novel, *Wait Until Spring, Bandini,* opens chapter 2. A discussion of the posthumously published works, *1933 Was a Bad Year* and "The Orgy," rounds out the chapter's examination of Fante's warmly rendered studies of boyhood. The protagonists of the novels discussed in chapter 3 are all young men trying to become authors in depression-era Los Angeles. That chapter examines *The Road to Los Angeles, Dreams from Bunker Hill,* and Fante's best-known and most critically admired novel, *Ask the Dust.* Chapter 4 analyzes *Full of Life, The Brotherhood of the Grape,* and "My Dog Stupid." Those three works feature protagonists who are making do with adulthood's stresses and disappointments with bitter humor and verve. A final chapter assesses the state of current Fante scholarship and considers Fante's contributions overall.

The family and matters Italian are among the great preoccupations of Fante's work and the cultural mediations that the characters attempt exhibit Fante's heightened sensitivity to the complexities of the immigrant experience. It is worth taking a brief detour here to discuss relevant theories of ethnicity before embarking on a discussion of Fante and his works. David Fine acknowledges these ethnic contestations in his assessment of Fante's 1952 novel *Full of Life:* "The father-son conflict is transformed into a battle between the stubborn peasant father . . . and the successful assimilated son, embarrassed and annoyed by the old man's persistence in old ways" (Fine 1993, 161). Fine's recognition of the struggles between worlds old and new applies to Fante's works overall, where matters Italian are similarly aligned with the past and contrasted with an American present. It is useful to consider critic Werner Sollors's theories of ethnicity in this light.[2] Sollors argues that *though assimilation is the antithesis of ethnicity, these notions—of ethnicity and assimilation—are, in fact mutually dependent* (Sollors, xiv; italics added). In Sollors's view, it is only when there is a threat of losing *ethnicity* at the hand of *assimilation* that ethnicity becomes formalized or identified. Repeatedly, Fante's characters undergo a process of ethnic realization just when they feel themselves on the verge of assimilation. In *The Brotherhood of the Grape*, especially, it is the impending death (loss) of the father (connection to Italy/ethnicity) that causes an awakening of ethnic identification in the assimilated son. Clearly, this is charged territory, and in keeping with Fante's general style, these novels do not shy from depicting the energetic battles that ensue from these cultural and ethnic conflicts.

Thomas Ferraro's study on immigrant novels, *Ethnic Passages: Literary Immigrants in Twentieth-Century America,*[3] does not discuss Fante specifically but the conclusions he makes about immigrant writers are very relevant to Fante. Ferraro identifies a common trait for immigrant and ethnic writers; when they choose to be a writer, there ensues a "profound degree of cultural self-distancing" (Ferraro, 9). This self-distancing has many ramifications, and Ferraro goes on to give a character sketch of ethnic writers: "When individuals from genuinely illiterate or impoverished backgrounds become writers, they pass through or somehow short-circuit far more common and reliable forms of mobility, freely choosing the special kind of marginalization involved in becoming a writer. Typically, they are alienated from family and friends of their youth; they marry or cohabitate outside the ethnic group; they live not in downtown ghettos but uptown, in ethnic suburbia, or most likely, in polyethnic bohemias catering to artists and intellectuals" (Ferraro, 9). Point for point, Ferraro's synopsis of ethnic writers rings true for Fante's life and echoes the experiences of his protagonists. One of the more relevant points of Ferraro's analysis is the discussed significance of what electing a writing career means for immigrant authors. Fante's fatherhood novels enact these conflicts; the Italian father's bewilderment, and sometimes disgust, at his son's chosen career (that of being a writer, instead of taking up the father's stonemason's trade) merges with and compounds the myriad cultural distances separating their generations. For Fante, ethnicity and family dynamics are inextricably overlaid.

If we conceptualize Fante's works in the way in which this study has arranged them—books of youth (chapter 2), of young manhood (chapter 3), and of fatherhood (chapter 4)—the identification with matters Italian echoes the paradigm often plotted for children of immigrants (and the protagonists of Fante's novels are, without fail, the sons of an Italian immigrant). The books of youth—particularly *Wait Until Spring, Bandini* and *1933 Was a Bad Year*—are deeply invested in the Italian Old Country that characterizes home. The books of young manhood—

especially *Ask the Dust*—are caught up in the American experience where the protagonist is largely independent of his family and living in the city of his dreams. The books of fatherhood discussed in the fourth chapter—*Full of Life, The Brotherhood of the Grape,* and "My Dog Stupid"—demonstrate a return to characteristics specifically identified as Italian. These fatherhood novels also signal a new respect for a past that the protagonists had convinced themselves was irrelevant to their American lives.

Acknowledgments

My special thanks go to Joyce Fante for the afternoons spent answering my many questions about her husband and his work; to Jim Fante for tracking down photographs of his father; to Alida Allison of San Diego State University for her expertise and unflagging encouragement; to Michael Cowan and Paul Skenazy of the University of California, Santa Cruz, for their support of this project; to Emily Klein for her editing flair and excellent tea; to Geoffrey Dunn for sharing his knowledge; to Dana Gioia for his guidance; to Eileen Dalton, Gregg Marrama, Anouchka Mari, Dina Burg, Tony Saavedra, Paul Lafferty, LaRae and John D'Amico, and all the other kind souls who gave sanctuary to me and my computer during the composition of this book; to Lisa Guerrero, Chris Shinn, Casey Kile, Maria Elena Caballero-Robb, Jeremy Rubenstein, Kristen Brookes, David Shorter, and all my colleagues at the University of California, Santa Cruz; to the many Fante scholars who shared generously their articles and ideas; to my editors at Twayne, Joseph Flora and Anne C. Davidson; to my San Pedro homies; to Jane Solie, the Yorgs, June Smith, and Tamara Johnson for their contributions; to the Troyer-Zicarelli family for their computer know-how and unparalleled company; and to my family, Judy, John, and Johnny, for everything else.

Material by John Fante from *Ask the Dust*; *The Brotherhood of the Grape*; *Dreams from Bunker Hill*; *Full of Life*; *1933 Was a Bad Year*; *The Road to Los Angeles*; *Wait Until Spring, Bandini*; *West of Rome*; *John Fante and H. L. Mencken: A Personal Correspondence, 1930–1952*; and *John Fante: Selected Letters 1932–1981* reprinted with the permission of Black Sparrow Press.

Chronology

1909   John Fante born in Denver, Colorado, on April 8, the first child of Nick and Mary Fante, Italian stonemason and Italian American homemaker. Grows up in Boulder where he attends public and parochial schools. Attends St. Regis, a Jesuit secondary school. Briefly attends the University of Colorado.

1930   Moves to the harbor area of Los Angeles. Works as a day laborer on the docks. Begins lengthy correspondence with H. L. Mencken of the *American Mercury*.

1931   Briefly attends Long Beach City College.

1932   Mencken accepts Fante's "Altar Boy" for publication in the *American Mercury*. Mencken publishes two other stories by Fante before the year's end.

1933   Moves to downtown Los Angeles where he works odd jobs. Begins lifelong friendship with activist-lawyer-author Carey McWilliams, through whom he is introduced to Hollywood screenwriters. Alfred Knopf contracts him to write a novel, *Pater Doloroso*.

1934   Begins working for Hollywood studios while writing his fiction. Publishes short stories; finishes *Pater Doloroso* (never published).

1935   Drafts *The Road to Los Angeles* (published posthumously in 1985).

1936   Works for Hollywood studios and publishes stories in premier magazines. In November attends the Western Writers Conference in San Francisco, a convention of artists and labor leaders.

1937   Spends most of the year living with his parents in the Sacramento Valley town of Roseville. Marries Stanford graduate, editor, and writer Joyce Smart.

1938   Moves back to Los Angeles with wife. First novel, *Wait Until Spring, Bandini,* published by Stackpole Sons.

1939 *Ask the Dust* published by Stackpole Sons.

1940 *Dago Red,* a collection of his published short stories, published by Viking Press.

1942 First of four children born to the Fantes. During the 1940s Fante attempts and eventually abandons a novel on the Filipino experience in California. Works for Orson Welles on *It's All True* (released posthumously) and other prominent directors. Writes news copy for the Office of War Information.

1950 Father dies.

1952 *Full of Life* published by Little, Brown and Company.

1955 Diagnosed with diabetes.

1956 H. L. Mencken dies.

1957 *Full of Life* released as a successful movie (screenplay adaptation by Fante).

1958–60 Success of *Full of Life* brings Fante more and better screenwriting assignments. Spends much of the late 1950s writing screenplays on location in Europe (principally Italy and France).

1969 Effectively retires from screenwriting. Writes novella "My Dog Stupid" (published 1986 in *West of Rome*).

1977 *The Brotherhood of the Grape* published by Houghton Mifflin.

1978–79 Increasingly ill with diabetes; loses eyesight and then legs.

1980 Black Sparrow Press reprints acclaimed *Ask the Dust.*

1981 Flush with the success of *Ask the Dust,* dictates his last novel, *Dreams from Bunker Hill,* to his wife.

1982 *Dreams from Bunker Hill* published by Black Sparrow Press.

1983 *Wait Until Spring, Bandini* republished by Black Sparrow Press. May 8, John Fante dies.

1985 Posthumously discovered novels, *The Road to Los Angeles* and *1933 Was a Bad Year,* published by Black Sparrow Press, as well as *The Wine of Youth: Selected Stories of John Fante.*

1986   *West of Rome* published by Black Sparrow Press.

1989   *John Fante and H. L. Mencken: A Personal Correspondence,
        1930–1952* published by Black Sparrow Press; *Ask the
        Dust* on bestseller lists in France. Film version of *Wait
        Until Spring, Bandini* released.

1991   *John Fante: Selected Letters 1932–1981* published by
        Black Sparrow Press.

1996   California State University, Long Beach, hosts a John
        Fante conference. Scholars from across the United
        States and Europe attend.

2000   Three scholarly books on Fante published including
        this one, Richard Collins's *John Fante: A Literary Por-
        trait* (Toronto: Guernica Editions), and Stephen
        Cooper's *Full of Life: A Biography of John Fante* (New
        York: Farrar, Straus, and Giroux).

Chapter One
John Fante's Remarkable Life

John Fante's is a dramatic life story of humble beginnings, ambition, early successes, tenacity, hope, disappointment after disappointment, and, in the end, more acclaim than he had allowed himself to expect.

Readers in search of the John Fante behind his fiction are fortunate to have available to them the two volumes of letters that Black Sparrow Press has published. In addition to being lively reading for their own sake, the letters are a vital source of information about what Fante thought; aside from a single published interview,[1] the letters are the only primary materials available. In these two collections, Fante's ideas about writing and the times in which he lived are vividly recorded. The first collection—*John Fante and H. L. Mencken: A Personal Correspondence*[2]—presents the letters exchanged between Fante and Mencken over the course of 25 years, beginning when Fante was a young man trying to get published in Mencken's *American Mercury*. In the early letters, such as this one from 1932, it is clear that Fante very much plays the role of an apprentice seeking guidance and validation from Mencken, his chosen mentor: ". . . you're the only person whom I know whose acumen I respect. I get endless unsolicited advice from people who read a lot and plan to write, but never do it. They give me a pain in the neck" (*Correspondence*, 25). By the time the letters end in 1952, Fante himself was a seasoned author.

The second volume—*John Fante: Selected Letters 1932–1981*[3]—collects the remainder of Fante's extant letters, the vast majority of which are dated from the 1930s and 1940s. Many from the early years are addressed to his parents, principally his mother, and describe his life in Los Angeles during the depression. Letters to Carey McWilliams, the lawyer-author-activist, comprise much of the remainder of Fante's letters, which register the novelist's views on literature and the social movements and events that affected the two men. Fante's letters show that he could be brash, funny, and emotional, qualities that all of his protagonists share. *John Fante: Selected Letters 1932–1981* also contains some of Fante's travel sketches as well as a month's worth of diary entries from 1940. As a whole, the volume portrays Fante's lively perspective on his personal and literary life.

On April 8, 1909, John Thomas Fante was born to Nick Fante, an Italian stonemason, and Mary Capolungo Fante, an Italian American from Chicago. John was the eldest of four children raised in Boulder, Colorado. Fante's youth was marked by conflicts that reappear in his fiction, including grinding poverty and problems between his very devoutly Roman Catholic mother and his drinking, gambling, and philandering father. That Nick Fante was also an exceptional stonemason did not alleviate the family's poverty but did instill in John Fante an abiding admiration for his father's talent. Though the Fantes were not a reading family, they were storytellers. Years later, John's widow Joyce recalled that patriarch Nick Fante "loved to tell stories, but they were always overblown and he was always the hero of it all."[4] The Fantes were outspoken and given to both blistering arguments and effusive expressions of love. The openness with which the Fantes communicated is evident in John's candid letters to his mother, where he confides in her his writing struggles, his love affairs, and even his getting circumcised in his early twenties.

The Fantes' poverty meant that they were usually indebted to local merchants and banks, and this was a shame that John felt keenly. He also felt a certain social ostracism at being not only poor but also Italian in the small, Anglo Boulder. According to Joyce Fante, Fante was painfully aware that during his youth and early manhood, Italians were considered by the Anglo mainstream to be an inferior ethnicity ("Interview"). At his secondary school he was one of the few Italians and was often referred to as a "wop" and a "dago," even by the priests who taught there ("Interview"). Fante's physical appearance, however, seemed more textbook American than Italian. He was described by his friend Ross Wills as having a "mop of sandy-reddish hair, and as impudent a freckled face as might ever have come out of any small American town."[5] The sense of being both a cultural and economic outsider would characterize every combative protagonist Fante ever created.

As a youth, Fante attended local parochial schools and then Denver's St. Regis College, a Jesuit-run boy's boarding school. He spent his free time playing baseball and was an outstanding pitcher, but his short stature prevented him from pursuing a career in the major leagues. Another talent of Fante's—that for writing—became apparent after he took up reading canonical literature, and his teachers urged him to continue writing. For a brief time after high school, Fante attended the University of Colorado (located in his hometown), but he quickly decided that he was not suited to academia. Fante was anxious to head for the West Coast, to leave home and live on his own.

In 1930 Fante hitchhiked with a friend to Southern California to pursue a life on his own, but he was not so quickly free of his family. His father abandoned wife Mary and the children for another woman, so Mary packed up the kids and moved to Wilmington, California, in the Los Angeles harbor area, to live near her brothers and John. As the eldest son, John worked at a variety of jobs to provide for his newly arrived, and more destitute than usual, family. About this period of his life, Fante wrote to Mencken that he "did a pretty swell job of keeping alive my ma and the kids. I had more than one job, I had twenty-four of them, from hotel clerk to stevedore" (*Correspondence*, 30). His experiences with these various harbor jobs provided much of the material for *The Road to Los Angeles* (written 1934; published 1985). He was also writing fiction during this time, though his work and family responsibilities limited his output. Within a year of their separation, Fante's parents reconciled and moved the family to Roseville, California, a small town near Sacramento.

With his family a solid day's travel away from Los Angeles, Fante was finally on his own, and he remained in the harbor area, writing stories, working odd jobs, and even managing to take English classes at Long Beach City College (*Letters*, 21). He lived with his girlfriend, a widowed music teacher 10 years his senior, as well as other friends and extended family (*Letters*, 23).[6]

Fante's peripatetic lifestyle did not dampen his desire to be an author, and in spite of what was a desperate poverty, his confidence in his writing never flagged for long. It is consistent with Fante's natural chutzpah that when he started sending off his stories for publication, he addressed them to Mencken's *American Mercury*, then one of the country's most prestigious literary journals. It turned out to be the best place for his work. Mencken had worked with, or published work by, Sinclair Lewis, Theodore Dreiser, James M. Cain, and James Farrell. Fante must have intuited that Mencken would be interested in his stories, and the editor indeed was open to hearing from new authors who captured a hitherto underdocumented slice of American life. For two years Fante sent Mencken stories and long, tortured letters raving about prose and life, letters judiciously and succinctly answered with good humor, encouragement, and advice. In one early letter (March 1931), Mencken assuages the young writer's anxiety over having his stories rejected:

"Dear Mr. Fante: Thanks very much for your pleasant note. . . . I hope you don't allow yourself to be discouraged. Getting a start in writing is a slow business, but if you are persistent you'll succeed" (*Correspondence,* 19). After many rejections, Fante's "Altar Boy" was accepted by the *American Mercury* in August 1932. Mencken accepted two other short stories by Fante before 1932 was over.[7]

Mencken proved to be an effective mentor for Fante, by guiding him into print and later by helping him through the processes and hazards of book publishing. The young author proved a quick study. Within a year of being published in Mencken's magazine, Fante had a publishing contract with Alfred Knopf for a novel (*Correspondence,* 48) and a New York agent. This auspicious beginning did not, however, continue smoothly, as Fante had trouble writing a book that Knopf liked. The author's first attempt, *Pater Doloroso* in 1934, was rejected by Knopf. Fante looked again to Mencken, who comforted Fante by relating that he advised young writers "to scrap their first two or three book manuscripts. Many a man has been ruined by being published prematurely. After you have done two novels you'll be able to make a third that will be ten times better than either" (*Correspondence,* 77). This scrapping of subsequent book manuscripts Fante was forced to do.

Flush with his first story acceptances, Fante moved in 1932 from the harbor area to Los Angeles, where he took up residence at a hotel on Bunker Hill near downtown (*Letters,* 21). During this time Bunker Hill was not the posh neighborhood it had been; it was described later by Mike Davis as a place of "epic dereliction."[8] Fante's descriptions of Bunker Hill are less apocalyptic than Davis's, but there is certainly an element of "epic dereliction" to Fante's Bunker Hill. In a 1941 essay, Ross Wills wrote a portrait of his friend's early days in Los Angeles. Wills depicts Fante's Bunker Hill hotel as "swarming with involuntarily-retired orange pickers from the East, bus boys, the frowzier streetwalkers, and poor and old and defeated people from all over the world" (Wills, 86). Wills describes Fante as fascinated with his neighbors and hosting, in the young writer's small room, "a communal life-story telling contest, while John egged [his visitors] on and listened and commented sympathetically" (Wills, 87). Fante's experiences during this time, associating with people as poor and dreamy as himself, as well as the sharp impressions of Los Angeles's downtown, form the core of *Ask the Dust* (1939) and—many years later—*Dreams from Bunker Hill* (1982). Two chapters of *The Brotherhood of the Grape* (1977) also contain a brief, but penetrating, portrait of 1930s Bunker Hill.

From his hotel room, Fante wrote short stories for the *American Mercury* and, after Mencken strongly encouraged him to do so, he published in other magazines including the *Atlantic Monthly* and the *Saturday Evening Post.* He wrote and rewrote novel drafts for Knopf and lived the life of a struggling artist. Finding any work was still difficult for Fante in Los Angeles. Every letter he wrote in 1932 discusses work or money. In one letter to his mother he philosophically describes his penury as necessary for his art:

> These days money is scarce. Every penny is huge. I'm spending my time writing until something develops for the better. This is the best thing I can do at the moment, since I'm determined to make my living by writing and no other way. Every writer has to do a certain amount of starving before he is worth a damn. He has to experience the hard things as well as the easy, and I'm at the moment getting my share of the harsh side of this business of living. Don't worry about me. I can always manage somehow. (*Letters,* 31)

Fante managed by working in restaurants and for an ice company and taking any job he could find.

The early 1930s also found Fante becoming acquainted with individuals who would form the most pivotal relationships of his life. He met lawyer-author-activist Carey McWilliams through Mencken's recommendation. Fante and McWilliams were fast friends.[9] McWilliams had a prolific legal and writing career that was rooted in his activist's enthusiasm for human and civil rights.[10] The head of the California Division of Immigration and Housing, McWilliams also chaired the Sleepy Lagoon Murder Trial Defense.[11] McWilliams's culminating achievement in letters was becoming editor in chief of the *Nation* (after editing a special issue on civil liberties) in the early 1950s, a post he held for 20 years.[12] But in the 1930s especially, from the time when he and Fante first met, McWilliams was regularly engaged in liberal politics.

McWilliams introduced his new friend not only to political circles (in which Fante was never much interested) but also to the core of Los Angeles's working writers. It was through McWilliams that Fante met authors Louis Adamic and Jo Pagano, screenwriter Ross Wills, and many others. Fante was quickly accepted as a fellow writer, and his talent must have been apparent to many people: in the latter half of 1932 Wills was trying to aid Fante in his search for studio work while Maxim Leiber,[13] the influential New York agent, was shopping his fiction to magazines and publishing houses (*Letters,* 34). By the end of 1932, Fante's prospects for making a living were improving. His letters home

at Christmas speak not of possible jobs hauling ice, or on the boat to
Catalina, but of writing work at the motion picture studios.

After visiting and meeting with studio scenarists for the first time,
Fante excitedly described to his mother the lucrative opportunities in
Hollywood: "The prices paid for short stories out there took my breath
away. They will pay me from $500 to $2000 for a good scenario" (*Letters*, 27). To understand how astronomical those sums were, Seamus
Cooney, editor of Fante's collected letters, explains: "We need to multi-
ply [those amounts] by at least 15 to 20 to get the rough equivalent in
today's money" [$7,500 to $40,000] (*Letters*, 38).

But almost as soon as he cashed his first check from Hollywood,
Fante understood that Hollywood's working conditions were going to
put in limbo his dreams of being a great author. In a letter home he
assessed the pitfalls of writing for the motion picture industry: "I don't
like working for the movies . . . I am not in a good position here. I may
be out of a job tomorrow. . . . You never know where you are, and at any
moment you can expect to be fired. That goes not only for me but for
every other writer" (*Letters*, 85–86). The uncertainty and unpredictable
nature of the movies plagued Fante's conscience and interrupted sustained concentration on his fiction. And Fante found it difficult to cope
with the seemingly arbitrary destiny that governed the production of
films. As is customary, most of Fante's work never made it to the screen
as he had written it, if it made it to the screen at all. In spite of Hollywood's detrimental impact on his serious writing, Hollywood's mone-
tary possibilities as a way out of poverty were ultimately too alluring to
pass up; Fante eventually made excellent money at the studios. But as
work in Hollywood was never reliable and Fante was an extremely poor
financial manager, and because of the financial needs of his family in
Roseville (for whom Fante remained partially responsible), his financial
woes, even when he was working, were chronic.

Hollywood, at that time, was employing a good many great authors.[14]
While working for the studios, Fante met Nathanael West, John Steinbeck, William Saroyan, F. Scott Fitzgerald, and William Faulkner. At
the end of his life, Fante recalled Faulkner as a friend and a "nice man.
Distinguished, a southern gentleman" (Pleasants, 93). Fante described
the kind of writing Faulkner did in Hollywood: "When he wrote a
screenplay, it was something to behold, because he wrote everything. He
wrote it like a novel, and when he finished, it would be about 350 pages
long" (Pleasants, 93). In a 1974 letter, Fante remembered that Faulkner's
well-known drinking problems meant that "executives would not trust

him to deliver [his work]. In 1943 or '44 I worked [with him] at Warners . . . My salary was $450 a week. Would you believe that Faulkner was only earning $250 per week?" (*Letters*, 294).

In his off-hours Fante caroused in the social haunts of his fellow literati: the Stanley Rose bookstore and restaurant-bars such as Ciro's, Musso-Frank, and the Garden of Allah (*Letters*, 182). The sense of both unified community and competition that existed among these authors is evident in Fante's collected letters. Authors assisted each other, as when Saroyan and Steinbeck wrote letters of support for Fante's 1940 Guggenheim Fellowship application (*Letters*, 182).[15] Fante was close with Saroyan especially.[16] That Fante's relationship with Saroyan was particularly gregarious is indicated by a letter arranging a meeting in San Francisco. He opens the letter to Saroyan: "Dear Tiger Saroyan, Wildcat Willie the Wow" (*Letters*, 152).[17]

Despite his immersion in the Hollywood environment and his 30-odd years of working in the "lucrative hell of studio screenwriting," Fante never considered himself a screenwriter.[18] As his wife recounted: "The only thing that writing scenarios did was bring him large sums of money during the long periods when he wasn't writing novels" (Domercq, 2). These trying personal and professional experiences in Hollywood screenwriting are recounted in *Full of Life* (1952), *Dreams from Bunker Hill* (1982), and "My Dog Stupid" (1986). Toward the end of his life, Fante felt compelled to defend the reasons why he had stayed in Hollywood for so long, and he remarked on this in a 1972 letter to Carey McWilliams: "I am always accused of forsaking my writing for the Hollywood glitter and gold. Nobody . . . bothers to consider that I had a family to maintain. . . . That I worked as a screenwriter is treated as if I had had a bout with the clap. If, on the other hand, I had pumped gas instead, or been a bricklayer, the ensuing glamour would have immortalized me" (*Letters*, 294). Fante's bitterness for his Hollywood years subsided at the very end of his life when he was earning such tremendous reviews from readers of his fiction. Gerald Managan sees Fante as an author putting to rest conflicted feelings over his tenure in Hollywood when he says that *Dreams from Bunker Hill*'s "surface wryness does not distract us from the sense that it crystallizes a few decades of frustration" (Managan, 303). Although Hollywood stood between Fante and his fiction for decades, the attention that Hollywood has since paid to his novels has earned him further acclaim.

When a young man in Hollywood, Fante did not limit his social circle to Hollywood's well-paid, if frustrated, hacking screenwriters. Los

Angeles had a small but thriving bohemian group in which Fante mingled. A 1936 letter Fante wrote to McWilliams from Roseville (during
one of Fante's brief stints living there) gives an impression of the crowd
to which they belonged:

> I finally heard from Ross [Wills]. He is very busy with his own studio
> work in addition to work on an original story. Today I received four
> copies of Pacific Weekly with our story printed therein. What do you
> know about Elsa Gidlow? . . . I see she is a frequent contributor to the
> weekly. Her sister Ruby seemed very nice in the mails. The last I heard
> from her was a card from Canada. Saroyan—now that he is in the movies
> [Frank] Fenton calls him William The Conquered—seems to be slipping.
> His piece in the weekly was quite bad. I saw of course the review by your
> red protégé Esther. What did she finally do with her plan for the Wasser-
> mann biography? It's a job to scare even Lytton Strachey. (*Letters*, 133)

Clearly, Fante belonged to a diverse and creative social set. His socializa-
tion into this literary in crowd testifies to Fante's personal adaptability:
he was, after all, a newcomer to letters, to California, and to Hollywood.

Though never himself a member of any political organization or move-
ment, Fante's social circle was very political, especially during the thirties
and forties. It is worth pausing here to discuss Fante's views on politics, for
he was often outspoken in his skepticism when those around him were
activists, and he was often taken to task for his views. In 1936 Fante
accompanied McWilliams to the Western Writer's Conference in San
Francisco, which Fante recounted to Mencken—with a suitably Menckian
skepticism—as being equal parts committed activism and fashion show.
The latter element of the conference was embodied by Dorothy Parker,
who disappointed Fante since she displayed none of her talent for "cutting
people down": "Dorothy Parker, who is evidently 'in sympathy' with the
proletariat, breezed into the hall wearing a Hollywood fur coat that must
have cost easily two grand, and promptly the poor red women sighed
adoringly" (*Correspondence*, 106). Fante also ridiculed McWilliams's selflessness at the conference. Fante wrote to Mencken: "After three days of
slavery for those longhairs they made him editor of a dozen different pam-
phlets, programs, brochures, magazines, and papers . . . [as well as] chair-
man of fifty different committees" (*Correspondence*, 107). Actually,
McWilliams's commitments and contributions were so voluminous that
Fante's hyperbole was probably not too far off the mark.

Though Fante caricatured most aspects of the conference to the more
conservative Mencken, he did feel gratified to meet and talk with Harry

Bridges, the Australian-born labor leader of the International Long-shoreman's and Warehouseman's Union (a year later, in 1937, Bridges became president of the ILWU, and he served as such for 40 years). Fante reported to Mencken: "He's a good man for the stevedores: one of those rare people who won't sell out under any circumstances. He must be forty-two, a tall bundle of nerves, humorless as a stomach pump" (*Correspondence*, 108). It is fitting that the politically reluctant Fante responded to this politically savvy man on the basis of the longshoreman's personal—not political—incorruptibility.

Fante's skepticism of ideologies, or political philosophies, and his reluctance to be associated with political organizations was fueled by an intense commitment to his individuality. Fante's desire to maintain his independence reappears throughout his letters to McWilliams and contrasts sharply with McWilliams's social activism. It would be fascinating to know how McWilliams responded to communiqués from his friend such as: "The storm is coming. Christ knows what I'll do then, but you can be sure I'll regard the safety of John Fante very highly. I'll go fascist if they leave me alone and let me write what I please. I'll go red for the same reason. . . . In other words, the side that does as much for me will do as much for mankind, and that side is where I go" (*Letters*, 135). One has to presume that such reductive political theory is written primarily to get a rise out of the politically invested McWilliams. But the frequency with which such sentiments of shameless self-interest are expressed in his letters suggests that there is something more to them than mere taunting.[19]

As the letters indicate, Fante had little patience for movements that asked the individual to subsume personal singularity for the sake of a collectivity. Much of Fante's personality was predicated on difference, on being Italian American in an Anglo mainstream, on being Catholic in a Protestant country, on being a westerner trying to succeed in literary publishing (an east coast establishment). His position of outsider was a fundamental aspect of Fante's identity, and it gave him something to bring to the table. Fante perceived Marxism, for instance, as a direct threat to his identity (his perceived difference) because it elided ethnicity and nationality for the interests of economic class. This conflict was very clearly articulated when Fante accompanied McWilliams to another convention—this one in Fresno (an agricultural hub of California)—the 1940 Conference for Democratic Action. Fante's diary entry documents what he perceived there: "The speeches were the same noises I heard as a boy . . . everyone [had] a job to fatten or protect . . . The whole thing was far from amusing. A gang of boobs running our state in that fashion is a damned dangerous situation. And of course the Communists were there, some openly so, and others that way by assumption. A disgruntled lot, as bad as the Democrats; a smug bunch of intellectuals, coldblooded and seditious" (Letters, 321–22). Fante was particularly irked by an exchange with McWilliams's secretary, Margaret Kalish, who responded to Fante's expressed interest in matters Italian with condescension: "When I told her I like many things Italian because my people were Italian, she pretended to find this a very quaint and primitive appreciation. She pretended to be dumbfounded by such an attitude. So shockingly unusual, etc. This got me down" (Letters, 322). His expressed self-interest and vague conservatism would serve Fante better when Hollywood began flushing out its leftists in the Red Scare of the late 1940s and early 1950s. Politics were always of minimal concern to Fante; though he wrote about socioeconomic circumstances similar to those that preoccupied Henry Roth, Steinbeck, and Farrell, Fante was no revolutionary and his works did not overtly challenge the socioeconomic system.

The middle 1930s found Fante continuing his nomadic lifestyle, moving at a rapid pace through different literary agents, movie studios, and neighborhoods. Many of the areas of Los Angeles that Fante called home during this time later figure as vital entities in his fiction: Bunker Hill, Venice, Long Beach, Hollywood, Terminal Island, and Santa Monica, for example. Also during this time Fante periodically moved to his parents' house in Roseville to escape the distractions of Hollywood screenwriting and the standard temptations of the big city. His writing suffered from other pitfalls in Roseville, notably the cramped living quarters and extreme weather that he sardonically described in a letter: "Very pleasant: an average temperature of 114 degrees. Ideal circumstances for terrific prosody" (Letters, 145).

These many relocations were initiated by fluctuations in income, up and down, and a frustrated author's search for the perfect place to write. The benefit of this itineration was that Fante gained an unequaled knowledge about California's stratified social climate and the distinctive communities of both the Los Angeles basin and the small towns of the rural Sacramento Valley. This understanding is evident in his novels' varied environments. Those works set in Los Angeles describe many Los Angeleses: the mainly immigrant working-class harbor and downtown areas, the Waspy middle-class Wilshire District, the both glitzy and tawdry Hollywood district, and, later, the affluent seaside community of Point Dume in Malibu.

In between bouts of writing for Hollywood, Fante was absorbed by a first and then, after that was rejected, a second novel for Knopf. *Pater Doloroso* and *In Our Time* (later retitled *The Road to Los Angeles*) were both rejected by the publisher. Fante was, of course, discouraged by this: he had spent five years not making deadlines, and after the advance money ran out, trying to write for Hollywood to eat and writing his novel in his extra time. During one of his stays in Roseville, Fante fell in love with a local girl. He and Joyce Smart, a Stanford graduate, an editor, and a poet, eloped to Reno in July of 1937 (Domercq, 1). He was thrilled by Joyce's intellectual energy, and they were deeply fond of one another though her comparatively well-off family did not approve of this son of an Italian bricklayer. When the couple eloped, Joyce was promptly disowned (her family later called a truce). John's connection to his wife's Anglo relatives meant that he would be forever linked to his earlier battles with the Anglo culture. Fante was able to find considerable humor and pathos in his and his wife's family situations, and the legacies of these tensions are expressed with vivid effect in *Full of Life* (1952), *The Brotherhood of the Grape* (1977), and "My Dog Stupid" (1986).

On another level, the marriage had many practical advantages, and these were not limited to Joyce's abiding belief in her husband's writing. Her talent for staying employed and managing finances enabled the couple to stay above the red line despite Fante's capricious runs at employment (both literary and hack). She also seemed to have a productive effect on his prose output: in the two years following their marriage he completed and published two novels, *Wait Until Spring, Bandini* (1938) and *Ask the Dust* (1939). Perhaps in homage to her belief in his talent, there is a wife figure in *Full of Life* (1952) who, in her commitment to her husband's literary work, resembles Joyce.

Fante wrote full time during the composition of these two novels, and not on screenplays.[20] Very few letters exist from the actual composition period of *Wait Until Spring, Bandini* and *Ask the Dust,* but the letters from the time immediately after the second novel's 1939 publication testify to Fante's confidence in his writing. He wrote to his parents about the thrill of seeing *Ask the Dust* in a Beverly Hills bookstore window on the day the novel was released (*Letters,* 154). In a letter to his cousin, Fante wrote: "a big, full book from me that succeeds will put me smacko among writers like Faulkner, Sinclair Lewis, Tom Wolfe" (*Letters,* 158).

Ask the Dust appeared to have every reason to sell well and bring Fante the acclaim to which he felt entitled. Publisher Stackpole Sons

(Fante and Knopf had by then parted ways) was encouraged by both the reviews and advance sales of *Ask the Dust* and had planned to "back the book heavily" (*Letters,* 154). There was talk of studios wanting the film rights to the novel (*Letters,* 158). Soon, though, the fanfare ended. Almost simultaneously with the novel's publication, Stackpole Sons became embroiled in a lawsuit brought against them on behalf of—of all people—Adolf Hitler: the publishing house had come out with an unauthorized edition of *Mein Kampf,* and the ensuing litigation proved cripplingly expensive. Within a year, Stackpole Sons was out of business (*Letters,* 150), and *Ask the Dust* started to gather dust on the bookshelf of American novels.

The 1940s was a decade complicated by war. Fante personally was distracted by thoughts of the draft, his work at the Office of War Information, and the responsibilities of a growing family (the Fantes' first child, Nicholas, was born in 1942) (*Letters,* 189). His literary publications were minor, limited to a collection of mostly previously published short stories in *Dago Red*[21] and nine short stories of varying quality that found print in the *Saturday Evening Post, Good Housekeeping,* and *Woman's Home Companion* (*Correspondence,* 161). Fante was dissatisfied with the quality of some of these pieces, and in a 1941 letter he expressly instructed Carey McWilliams *not* to read one of these stories: "*Don't watch for my piece 'Beautiful Bird' in Good Housekeeping. Peeeeeeeeewww!*" (*Letters,* 190). During this decade, Fante also began and abandoned three novels, including his never finished novel on the Filipino experience in California, which he would ultimately spend almost five years researching and writing (*Letters,* 189).

After the disappointment of not completing the Filipino novel—a story beyond his personal experience—Fante returned to what he knew best, and in so doing, he wrote the book that would bring him the most fame and financial success he would see in his lifetime. *Full of Life,* published in 1952, is a comic "autobiographical" portrayal of the birth of a young couple's first child. The novel was condensed by *Reader's Digest* and later made into a movie. Fante received an Academy Award nomination (1957) for his screenplay adaptation of the novel. With the revenues from *Full of Life,* the Fantes bought a ranch-style house on a bluff in Malibu where Joyce continued to live until very recently.

Full of Life is a product of the era in which it was written, when Hollywood's political and social climate—once fashionably progressive—was distinguished by a vogue conservatism. Nationwide, Americans after

World War II were preoccupied with political allegiance, and in large part, this interest was fueled by elected officials: Washington created the House Un-American Activities Committee to question allegiances. HUAC came to Hollywood, and a number of Hollywood actors, directors, and writers were called to Washington to testify about their politics and the politics of others. Fante worked with many writers who were forced to go subterranean to continue working after the infamous inquests: Edward Dmytryk, Dalton Trumbo, and Ben Hecht, all members of the Hollywood Ten, are the most noteworthy friends of Fante's who suffered from the era's panic.[22] In a 1951 letter Fante describes sitting in a Western Avenue bar, surrounded by soldiers, watching a fellow screenwriter testify before HUAC: "with the service men looking on . . . it was acutely painful because they hated the sight of her. . . . It was a very cruel business" (*Letters*, 229). Fante was a friend of Carlos Bulosan, the Filipino writer and labor activist and an avowed Communist. Years later, in a letter to McWilliams, Fante recounts being questioned by the FBI: "It was always necessary to hurdle these queries [concerning his knowledge of Communists] before I was permitted to take a job at MGM, RKO and Warner Brothers. The heart of the matter was always Carlos Bulosan" (*Letters*, 305). Though Fante never wrote to McWilliams about it, Joyce Fante remembers Fante being questioned about McWilliams as well ("Interview"). Fante was obviously not immune to the interrogations of the time, but his Hollywood livelihood does not appear to have been jeopardized.

Ben Pleasants has posited an ironic and tempting theory about Fante's apolitical stance, which he believes thwarted Fante's literary success in the 1930s when many critics had a strong Marxist-Leninist bent: Fante "wrote about working class people but he didn't raise the banner. So, he didn't fit and [the critics] didn't hold him up, because he wasn't one of their boys" (in Gordon, 27). This conjecture suggests that while Fante's apolitical predilection served him well commercially during the Red Scare, it may have hindered his initial critical success.

During the 1950s Fante spent most of his working time writing for the studios (*Letters*, 202). By the mid-1950s, he and Joyce had four children (Nicholas, Daniel, Victoria, James), and the arrival of the children meant that Hollywood's paychecks were welcomed. Soon Fante's literary production outside of Hollywood slowed and then stopped; after *Full of Life* and two short stories in 1952, he would not publish again for 25 years. In a later interview, Fante succinctly and self-deprecatingly assessed his life during that era: "I pissed away a few years of my life playing golf, reading, dallying with one novel and then another" (Pleasants, 95). In the middle of this publishing drought, Fante began, but did not finish, versions of *The Brotherhood of the Grape* and *1933 Was a Bad Year* (later published in 1977 and 1985, respectively) (*Letters,* 231).

Fante was a hot screenwriting property in the years following the Academy Award nomination he received for *Full of Life,* and the writer of choice for powerful directors. From 1958 to 1961 Fante worked on location in Naples, Rome, and Paris, completing screenplays for Dino De Laurentiis and other well-known directors (*Letters,* 269). In the late 1950s Joyce Fante joined her husband for a few weeks in Paris, which she later described as a whirlwind of transplanted Hollywood: there were "interminable forays of the nightclubs. Bill Saroyan was there, Orson Welles also" (Domercq, 3). Fante enjoyed these trips abroad, and they enabled him to visit Italy (his father's home country), which had had such an instrumental impact on his own life. In one letter to Joyce, Fante recounted his deep response to an Italian village: "The town is old, so very old. Strange, ancient odors come at you in ancient buildings, in alleys: the smell of so many hundreds of millions of people who have come and gone. Not really a disgusting odor, but curious, rather unpleasant, yet understandable" (*Letters,* 245). In a 1957 letter to Joyce he wrote of his fascination with the region: "Having been here a few days, I now know why they wanted me to come. We must make this story contemporary, in order to capture the fabulous richness of the present scene" (*Letters,* 244). Even after more than 20 mostly bitter and unproductive years in Hollywood, one still detects the engaged craftsman's eye in his desire to "capture the fabulous richness of the present scene."

The letters Fante addressed to his children during this time are particularly charming. Fante wrote to the two youngest children: "Dear Vicky and Jimmy: I thought you might like to know something about the children of Naples. In the first place, there are lots and lots of them, more children than you ever saw before—all shapes and sizes, from very tiny babies and super-tiny babies to big boys and girls. . . . They are very happy children. . . . They run in the streets, they climb church steps, they tumble around garbage cans. . . . They never seem to go to bed. From my hotel window I can see them down in the street, along the ocean wall, playing at midnight. But when I get up in the morning, there they are again, playing as hard as ever" (*Letters,* 248). In this series of letters Fante is at his fatherly best; his thoughtful descriptions of the sights, sounds, and people of Naples have all the drama of his fiction and are perfectly calibrated for his juvenile audience.[23]

Along with the professional adulation Fante was experiencing, the 1950s were a time when his health became a concern: he was diagnosed with diabetes in 1955 (*Letters, 223*). By watching his diet, he was able to keep the very serious effects of diabetes at bay for more than 25 years. In the 1960s Fante continued screenwriting and traveling to Europe for film projects. Letters home show that he maintained his sense of humor, even when he missed his family, as is illustrated in this amusing description of a trip to Italy: "Imagine traveling in one plane with 130 Italians! They scared hell out of me from the moment of departure in New York. My God, how they wailed, wept, flung arms around friends and relatives down to see them off! I got the awful feeling that we were all doomed" (*Letters, 269*). Fante's flair for capturing culture and local color are well documented in his letters home, though these impressions of Europe never found full expression in a literary format.

The late 1950s and early 1960s were the height of Fante's screenwriting career. Even at this high point, the satisfaction of being in demand and working under more lavish conditions was ultimately marred by the standard vagaries of movie projects: the many film ventures begun in Europe never saw completion. In an interview, Joyce Fante boiled down this era: "Beautiful times, but bitter disillusion at the end" (Domercq, 3).

Studio assignments tapered off in the latter part of the 1960s, until Fante was essentially retired. The frustrations of not being able to get a screenwriting assignment (ironic, since he never wanted one) form the core of a novella Fante began during the late sixties, "My Dog Stupid" (published in *West of Rome,* 1986). Because of the decline of available screenwriting work, his creative energy drove him to an available outlet: fiction. His overdue return to fiction resulted in renewed creativity for Fante. He had already begun sustained work on the story of his father's last days—*The Brotherhood of the Grape* (1977)—when a new generation of writers began to appear at Fante's Malibu doorstep, eager to express their admiration and wondering where he had been all these years.

Robert Towne, while researching 1930s Los Angeles for his *Chinatown* screenplay (1974), came across *Ask the Dust*.[24] Towne's readerly zeal for the novel soon turned into a desire to film the book, and he took out an option on *Ask the Dust* and began work on a screenplay adaptation. Francis Ford Coppola also became interested in Fante's writing. Coppola loved Fante's story of his father's final raucous days, so much so that he serialized *The Brotherhood of the Grape* in his short-lived *City Magazine.* Coppola optioned Fante's book and planned to direct the film version after the completion of his next project. With Towne and Coppola, two Hollywood lions, working on *Ask the Dust* and *The Brotherhood of the Grape*, respectively, Fante was beginning to think that maybe Hollywood would bear fruit for him after all.[25] In a letter Fante wrote: "A writer couldn't possibly have better auspices—two Academy award winners. . . . Needless to say, I am horribly cynical and expect the deal to blow up" *Letters,* 299). Fante's cynicism turned out to be prophetic. Coppola's next project was the infamously delayed epic *Apocalypse Now,* and Fante's story of his father was set aside. A movie version of *Ask the Dust* was also shelved. These blows were emotionally exhausting for the aging Fante, as Joyce Fante later described: "It was an enormous disappointment for John. He commenced during that period to become extremely ill and unhappy" (Domercq, 3). During the late 1970s, Fante began to suffer from the serious complications of diabetes, complications that finally resulted in the loss of both his legs and his eyesight.

To combat Fante's sunken spirits, his wife suggested that he write another novel—this time by dictation. According to Joyce Fante: "he would dictate the words and I would read them back the following morning. Then when the text was ready, I edited it, typed it, and sent it to his editor" (Domercq, 3). Thus, *Dreams from Bunker Hill,* his final novel, was written. It seemed that Fante would die writing, but generally unknown. But in 1980 fate, and the reverence of a longtime enthusiast of *Ask the Dust,* turned the trick.

Charles Bukowski, "Los Angeles' legendary rough beast slouching toward serious literature,"[26] referred to Fante's favorite protagonist, Arturo Bandini, in his book *Women.*[27] Bukowski's publisher, John Martin, became intrigued by the mention and read *Ask the Dust.* It struck a chord with Martin, and he agreed with Bukowski, who later wrote that *Ask the Dust* was "a wild and enormous miracle."[28] When Martin republished the novel under his Black Sparrow Press imprint in 1980, the novel had been out of print for 41 years. *Ask the Dust* stirred literary circles; the new generation of readers responded to the crack and sizzle in Fante's narratives and wondered why their grandparents had never mentioned John Fante. Reviews appeared in all the metropolitan newspapers and in magazines as widely read as *Vogue* and the *New Yorker.* Critics celebrated Fante's lyrical prose and his depictions of historically specific places, longed for and now long gone.[29] Reviews proliferated to the extent that they reached a point where writers were essentially reviewing not Fante's books but the phenomenal public interest in his work.[30] Fante's fame in the 1980s so outweighed the earlier attention paid to his literary output that interest in his work was less a renaissance than a birth.

In 1982 Fante finished his last novel, *Dreams from Bunker Hill,* and Black Sparrow published it the same year. In 1983 *Wait Until Spring, Bandini* (his first published novel) was republished. Fante's health was rapidly deteriorating, but his spirit was buoyed by the knowledge that his books were now widely read. It is fitting that a man who wrote such bittersweet novels would himself experience the same simultaneous mixture: bitter that the adulation came so late, but sweet triumph that he was alive to see his talent widely appreciated. John Fante died on Sunday, May 8, 1983.

As so often happens, Fante's death cemented his fame. Today all of Fante's books (nine altogether, four of which were published for the first time after his death) are in print with Black Sparrow Press, as are the two volumes of his collected correspondence. Black Sparrow Press is about to release a new collection of Fante's short stories, *The Big Hunger: 1932–1959* (scheduled for publication in spring 2000). A reckoning of Fante's tremendous international popularity is demonstrated by the many countries in which his books have been published, including Belgium, Brazil, England, France, Germany, Holland, Italy, Norway, Spain, and Sweden.[31] Fante's international popularity has been greater, actually, than his popularity in the United States. The French, who adore him as an American enfant terrible, thought enough of the Arturo Bandini sagas to keep Fante's name on the bestseller lists of *Le Point* and *Le Figaro* from 1989 to 1992.[32]

And Hollywood has been taking another look at those novels too. In 1989 no fewer than six of his novels had been optioned or were in some stage of production. Five years later, only one, *Wait Until Spring, Bandini,* found its way to the screen (1989). It seems that the characteristic capriciousness of motion picture projects has dogged Fante even after death. The agent for the Fante estate, Paul Yamamoto, reports that Peter Falk has purchased the rights to "My Dog Stupid," and that *1933 Was a Bad Year* has also been optioned. A documentary about Fante— directed and produced by Frank Spotnitz—is currently in the last stages of production.

After the flurry of attention in the 1980s, scholars began assessing Fante's work, and as time has gone on, scholarly attention has progressed from expressions of "Eureka!" to more sophisticated, sustained analyses of Fante's contributions to American letters. This was readily apparent at the John Fante Conference, sponsored by California State

University, Long Beach, in 1996 where scholars and general enthusiasts traveled from across the United States and Europe to meet and debate their ideas. An anthology of essays culled from the conference—*John Fante: A Critical Gathering*, edited by Stephen Cooper and David Fine (Fairleigh Dickinson University Press)—is forthcoming. In addition to this volume, two other book-length studies of Fante's work are set for publication. Cooper, the principal organizer of the conference, is completing work on his *Full of Life: A Biography of John Fante* (New York: Farrar, Straus, and Giroux, 2000). Richard Collins has finished his *John Fante: A Literary Portrait* (Toronto: Guernica Editions, 2000).

John Fante's visions of California and Colorado, his candid depictions of the negotiations of identity and ethnicity, and the lyricism with which he tells his lively stories ensure that discussions of his work will continue to challenge and interest readers.

Chapter Two
Boyhood in Colorado:
Wait Until Spring, Bandini;
1933 Was a Bad Year; "The Orgy"

Every 20 years or so, Fante's imagination compelled him to write a substantial piece on boyhood. Two novels and a novella are the fruits of that preoccupation. Considered together, *Wait Until Spring, Bandini,*[1] *1933 Was a Bad Year,*[2] and "The Orgy"[3] comprise a portrait of growing up Italian, Catholic, and poor in depression-era Colorado. *Wait Until Spring, Bandini,* Fante's first published novel, is where Arturo Bandini's saga begins. *1933 Was a Bad Year* shows Fante taking *Wait Until Spring, Bandini*'s childhood poverty and ethnic marginalization to its teenage consequence. Though divided by socioeconomic hierarchies, protagonist Dominic Molise and his best friend Kenny Parrish in *1933 Was a Bad Year* share a dream to leave their small Colorado town and become professional baseball players. "The Orgy" was published posthumously with "My Dog Stupid" as one of two novellas under the title *West of Rome.* One of Fante's most enigmatic works, "The Orgy" concerns the bad fortune of getting the gift of a gold mine. Avowedly autobiographical, these three works are thoughtful studies of boyhood in Colorado.

Wait Until Spring, Bandini

Wait Until Spring, Bandini is a novel of poetry and brio predicated on the sweeping emotions of passionate familial and romantic love. The novel's vigor was eloquently, if inadvertently, remarked upon by author and critic Louis Adamic. When he reviewed the novel, Adamic mistakenly put an exclamation mark at the end of the title, rendering it *Wait Until Spring, Bandini!*[4]

At the time *Wait Until Spring, Bandini* was issued, Fante was a respected short story writer whose works had been published in the nation's foremost magazines, such as the *American Mercury,* the *Saturday Evening Post,* and the *Atlantic Monthly.* It was his success in the short

19

story trade that gained Fante his 1933 book contract from Alfred A. Knopf. Writing his first novel consumed Fante for years: nearly every existing letter from 1933–1938 remarks on the alternate frustration and elation he experienced as he was watching the pages of his novel stack up or throwing away drafts and reworking plotlines.

For this novel, Fante returned to the material that he had originally used to break into the magazine story trade, his Colorado childhood. *Wait Until Spring, Bandini* is probably a reworked version of an earlier, now-lost manuscript Fante had called *Pater Doloroso*. Fante had written that *Pater Doloroso* chronicled an Italian American family in Colorado and their troubles with birth control, a practice their Roman Catholic religion forbids (*Letters*, 115). Fante repeated this story line in a 1936 letter to Carey McWilliams: "It is the tale of a fourteen year old boy who writes of the mysterious confusion in his home due to a conflict between his father and mother over an unending problem of birth-control" (*Letters*, 132).

If birth control had once been a main theme of *Wait Until Spring, Bandini*, it went underground. Fante probably found that a "straight piece of Italian-American writing" was rich enough to sustain a novel (*Letters*, 132). Sex permeates *Wait Until Spring, Bandini*, perhaps as a vestige of the birth control theme of *Pater Doloroso*. The scenes of intimacy are plied with significance: love, power, insecurity, identity.

Like Arturo Bandini in all his incarnations, the events of *Wait Until Spring, Bandini* are charged and in equal measure endearing and off-putting. The book's tone is tragicomic, though the difficult situation of the Bandini family lends their few triumphs a certain dignity. They live in Rocklin, Colorado, a town of 10,000 residents, 30 miles from Denver. As poor as the snow is deep, the Bandinis tumble through the days leading up to Christmas. Mother Maria's prayers and the three sons' hopes for better days stoke the frustrations of Svevo, the father, who cannot find work to provide for groceries or rent, let alone Christmas presents. Svevo Bandini is a stonemason, a bricklayer, and a union man. But when the novel opens, the dire situation of the family indicates he has been unemployed for some time. Snow freezes the mortar he works with and Svevo describes his predicament simply: "No sunshine, no work" (*Wait*, 11). Svevo exacerbates his poverty by customary means: he drinks to forget it and gambles to get out of it. Also customarily, neither method solves his problems. Maria seeks solace in her deeply felt and incessantly practiced devotion to Catholicism and the Virgin Mary to whom she prays for strength and better fortune. Separated by very different temperaments and proclivities, Svevo and Maria nonetheless share a deep connection demonstrated in the first chapter's middle-of-the-night love-making scene. Sons Arturo, August, and Federico range in age from 14 to 8.[5] Though the other brothers are important characters and complete the family portrait, Arturo and his parents are the central focus of the book.

Described as a "miniature of his father, except for the mustache" (*Wait*, 31), Arturo shares with his father dreams of wealth and a preoc-cupation with dignity, coupled with a tendency toward self-sabotage. Arturo, though a miniature of his father in temperament, is not inter-ested in pursuing his father's stonemason's trade; Arturo dreams of zinging fastballs as a pitcher for the Yankees or Cubs. As it is for his father, winter is a hardship for Arturo; only when the ground is dry can he prove his mettle on the mound. During the winter months when baseball fields are frozen, Arturo fumes as he does his chores at home, his school lessons, and his duties as an altar boy. The only bright spot in his wintertime world is his love for Rosa Pinelli, a popular girl at school who does not encourage Arturo's pursuit. The season separates Svevo and Arturo from what makes them exceptional—stonemasonry and baseball—and as they await spring, they shadowbox their personal demons, skidding through the winter scenes disheveled and punch drunk with pride.

The family's strong connections, as demonstrated in the book's beginning chapter, are perforated at chapter's end by the announcement of the impending arrival of the formidable Donna Toscana, Maria's mother. She detests Svevo, routinely ridicules her daughter for marrying him, and scorns her grandchildren for being American. All are out-spokenly tormented by the thought of even an afternoon visit by Donna Toscana, but Svevo seethes quietly and uncharacteristically and, then, out the door he slips. He escapes to the residence hotel of Rocco Sac-cone, his friend from Italy. While with Rocco, Svevo is hired to work for Effie Hildegarde, a widow and the wealthiest woman in town. She wants him to fix her fireplace, a task which he performs ably, but she also pursues him as a lover. Though not much is said about Effie, her seduction of Svevo shows her loneliness and her preoccupation with the dangerous sexuality she perceives in him. Before long, they are sleeping together. Too guilty to go home, Svevo abandons his family, effectively leaving them without any income. Though she has no absolute proof, Maria is certain that Svevo is with another woman. As a result, Maria plunges into a deep and frightening depression and withdraws from her sons almost as entirely as Svevo abandons her. For a time, she lives in her rocking chair, "never moving, her elbow on the window sill, her chin in her hand as she watche[s] the cold deserted street" (*Wait,* 131). Soon she is a 24-hour somnambulist frequently found by her hungry and confused sons in the frigid coal shed or basement. On Christmas Eve, when her husband returns to reconcile, Maria reveals a will as fierce as her husband's and more frightening with its surprising intensity: she foists penance upon Svevo by clawing wounds onto his face.

Arturo's reaction to his father's affair is mixed: while he feels sympathy for his mother's plight and that of his own now fatherless existence, he also feels pride that his father has taken up with such a wealthy woman and thinks that under similar circumstances, he would do the same thing. But, as Svevo finds, bedding down with someone like Effie Hildegarde is not like simply taking a lover; the disparities in their social rank, their ethnicity, and their economic standing promote fascination between them, but bar understanding. Though they share moments of kindness, there remains an atmosphere of suspicion. In bed Svevo and Effie play out the fantasy of the brutally sexual peasant and the sex-starved, yearning if protesting, woman of gentility. During waking hours, they have almost nothing to say to each other. Neither the affair nor the fatherless house are situations that can continue indefinitely, and in the final pages of the story—with Svevo contrite and punished—appeasement is at hand. Maria cooks a big dinner in anticipation of Svevo's return, which she feels is imminent. To actualize that wish, Arturo goes to the widow's home to convince his father to return. Though Svevo hedges at first—"Maybe I'll come—and maybe I won't" (*Wait,* 261)—he welcomes the encouragement to reconcile. As father and son walk away from Effie Hildegarde's mountain house, her angry shouts of "You peasants!" and "You foreigners!" (*Wait,* 265) hang in the air like banners proclaiming the covert anger that had existed between Svevo and the widow all along. The disappointments of Christmas are over, spring is near, work and baseball to follow, dinner is on the table, and so the Bandinis survive another difficult winter.

Plot, Place, Narration

The plot of the novel is straightforward: family is threatened when father abandons them for another woman, making life very difficult for wife, sons, and husband too, and, after aborted attempts at peace, the family reconciles. The social context of the story enriches the uncomplicated plot with the mitigating circumstances of ethnicity and economic class. The telling of the story is also complex. The structure unfolds in self-contained chapters, linked but not successive in causality. For instance, Svevo is the core and star of the first chapter, but he drops out of the novel's action—except when his sons see him from afar—until chapter 7 when he returns home on Christmas Eve. The interregnum chapters—and they comprise much of the book—concern Arturo, his brothers, Maria, and what life is like for them in Svevo's absence. This technique of splitting and shifting spotlights gives each of the novel's three main characters—Svevo, Maria, and Arturo—the narrative space for the rich character development for which Fante's talent has been celebrated. Svevo, Maria, and Arturo are realistically deep and contradictory.

Fante is also celebrated for his place sketches. The snowy landscape of *Wait Until Spring, Bandini* puts his vibrant characters in sharp relief. Stripped of comforts, the Bandinis in winter are most vulnerable to themselves and to each other. For Arturo, while the snow literally puts his visions of baseball glory on ice, it also symbolizes the straits of his family. Walking downtown one evening after Svevo's abandonment, Arturo and his brother August catch a glimpse of Svevo driving with Effie, his arm resting on her shoulder. While Arturo is awed that his father could be so familiar with so wealthy a woman, the younger, more religious August feels moral repulsion. The boys walk home in a landscape richly symbolic. Taking a short cut through a pasture,

> [t]hey descended the crest of the railroad line and followed a faint trail which they themselves had made all that Winter in the comings and goings to and from school, through the Alzi pasture, with great sweeps of white on either side of the path, untouched for months, deep and glittering in the evening's birth . . . weary frozen cottonwoods strangled in the death pose of long winters on one side, and a creek that no longer laughed on the other. Beneath that snow was white sand once very hot and excellent after swimming in the creek . . . But in that twilight their father rode with Effie Hildegarde, and the silent white sweep of the pasture land was only a place for walking on a strange road to home. (*Wait*, 124)

Fante places considerable symbolic weight on snow. In the novel, the season's chill on the land very clearly parallels the burden that Svevo's abandonment puts on the family. To extend the metaphor, the inevitability of the season—that winter returns each year—raises the notion that the family's hardship and Svevo's abandonment will likewise be cyclical and, though expected, dreaded. In another allegorical depiction of nature, Svevo returns to Effie's house after Maria claws his face, the snowy landscape mirroring his misery: "A lonely road at the west end of Rocklin, thin and dwindling, the falling snow strangling it. Now the snow falls heavily. The road creeps westward and upward, a steep road. Beyond are the mountains. The snow! It chokes the world, and there is a pale void ahead, only the thin road dwindling fast. A tricky road, full of surprising twists and dips as it eludes the dwarfed pines standing with hungry white arms to capture it" (*Wait*, 170). Fante uses setting symbolically, and notably, his sketches are poetic and strongly evoked. As briskly paced as his writing is, it is worth reading slowly to grasp its poetic virtues.

The novel's third-person narration approximates the tones of the different characters, taking on the style of speech that the spotlighted character uses. The casual conversational tone of boyhood is especially well accomplished. In chapter 2, for example, Arturo's parochial school class is impatient to leave for the day. That teacher Sister Mary Celia is losing patience is indicated by the twitching of the eyelid housing her glass eye, a threat widely known through school lore. Nellie Doyle is giving a report to the class on Eli Whitney's cotton gin. Unfortunately for Jim Lacey and Eddie Holm, who are seated behind her, "her thin dress [is] caught between her buttocks." Lacey and Holm "[are] laughing like hell, only not out loud, at the dress caught in Nellie's buttocks. They [have] been told time and time again to watch out, if the lid over Old Celia's glass eye started jumping, but would you look at [Nellie] Doyle there!" (*Wait*, 46). The narrator here takes on the colloquialisms ("laughing like hell," "would you look at Doyle there!") that authenticate the story.

The dialogue between the Bandini brothers also evidences Fante's talent for getting right the nuances of boy-speak. Within August's succinct character sketch the narrator sounds like another boy: "August was ten; he didn't know much. Of course he knew more than his punk brother Federico, but not half so much as the brother beside him, Arturo, who knew plenty about women and stuff" (*Wait*, 30). In the following scene Arturo is attempting to strong-arm money out of August in exchange for information about sex.

> "What'll ya give me if I tell ya?" Arturo said.
> "Give you a milk nickel."
> "Milk nickel! What the heck! Who wants a milk nickel in winter?"

"Give it to you next summer."
"Nuts to you. What'll ya give me now?"
"Give you anything I got."
"It's a bet. Whatcha got?"
"Ain't got nothing." *(Wait,* 30)

In this conversation we see not only the nuances of the casual spoken English of schoolboys but also the machinations of childhood logic and negotiations. Fante's comedic timing is best appreciated in moments like these where children are running the show. Elsewhere, at the break-fast table when Federico, cowed by his father's glowering, tells his father that he does not want a motor boat (out of the question, in any case) if his father does not want him to have it, the narrator adopts the sarcasm of the monitoring Arturo: "Bandini nodded self-approvingly to his wife: here was the way to raise children, his nod said. When you want a kid to do something, just stare at him; that's the way to raise a boy. Arturo . . . sneered: Jesus, what a sap his old man was!" *(Wait,* 40). In these scenes it is clear that the book's sympathies are with the boys, particularly Arturo.

Boyhood

Wait Until Spring, Bandini in many ways approximates a coming-of-age story because Arturo and his brothers are so integral and because their lives—particularly Arturo's—undergo such dramatic changes. Critic Fred Gadarphé assesses the Bandini books as "episodic *bildungsromans*" and that classification works, to a point.[6] In a letter about an earlier draft of *Wait Until Spring, Bandini,* Fante communicated that the 14-year-old boy would be the main mouthpiece of the story: "The whole thing, told from the kid's point of view, has to be suggested of course, since he doesn't know what birth control is. It's a big subject which has all the force of every modern conflict, economic, moral, and physical. Whether the kid can swing it or not is another question" *(Letters,* 132). The point of view that Fante had earlier described as the boy's (a first-person narration) became in the novel's final version a third-person omniscient narrator. This narrator has complete access to the thoughts, feelings, and motivations of all the characters. That Arturo shares the mantle of protagonist with his parents means that *Wait Until Spring, Bandini* is not a true coming-of-age novel, not a *bildungsroman.* In any case, another critic recognized one of the novel's achievements when he ventured that *Wait Until Spring, Bandini* is "a serious study of boy nature."[7]

Another confirmation that *Wait Until Spring, Bandini* is not a conventional *bildungsroman*, though it is indeed a "serious study of boy nature," lies in the fact that Arturo's coming-of-age is, time and again, thwarted. For example, practicing for the Altar Boy's Christmas Banquet procession, Arturo is replaced by younger but taller brother, August, in the height-determined order (*Wait*, 124).[8] This is a wound to Arturo's ego, for which August will pay later with a bloody nose. Arturo's declension in the order retrogresses his physical rite of passage further from the appearance of a young adult.

Arturo's crush on Rosa Pinelli represents a second thwarted rite of passage. Arturo, true to his fluctuating emotions, alternately loves and hates Rosa because she is Italian American: "I am an Italian too, Rosa. Look, and my eyes are like yours. Rosa, I love you" (*Wait*, 116). He thinks of her as accompanying him when he becomes a big league pitcher, but when she proves unresponsive to his romantic overtures, he imagines her miserable and himself successful, happy, and the adored athlete of legions of Anglo blondes (*Wait*, 166). In one of Arturo's more manic moments, he wishes Rosa dead, and then immediately worries that she might very well be dead: "How did he know she wasn't dead by electrocution? That happened a lot. Why couldn't it happen to her? . . . Poor Rosa, so young and pretty—and dead" (*Wait*, 167). In a panic, he runs toward her house crying: "Oh Rosa, please don't die, Rosa. Be alive when I get there!" (*Wait*, 168). He sees on the Pinelli front door not a funeral wreath but a Christmas wreath and is relieved, but also a little disappointed, that his melodramatic fantasy is not true. Surprisingly, however, Rosa does die, after Christmas, of pneumonia. Upon her passing, Arturo feels a deep, steady grief that contradicts his customary emotional vacillations. When his mother hears of Rosa's death, she intuits Arturo's misery and slips him some coins to indulge himself at the soda fountain (*Wait*, 245). His grief prevents him from tasting the milk shake he orders and the arm's length kindness of a college girl there makes him think about Rosa's vibrancy, now extinguished. Back to the Pinelli house he goes, convinced that Rosa cannot be dead, "that it had been a false report, that she was alive and breathing and laughing like the college girl in the store, like all the girls in the world. Five minutes later, standing under the street lamp in front of Rosa's darkened house, he gazes in horror and misery at the white and ghastly thing gleaming in the night, the long silk ribbons swaying as a gust of wind caresses them: the mark of the dead, a funeral wreath" (*Wait*, 246). The event transpires with little editorializing: Arturo's anguish is enough. These three difficult experiences—being short for his age, being rebuffed by Rosa, and Rosa's death—converge poignantly when Sister Mary Celia deems Arturo too short to be a pallbearer at Rosa's funeral (*Wait*, 250).

Arturo is repeatedly challenged by disappointments and obstacles. As the main boy in *Wait Until Spring, Bandini,* his depiction seems to imply an overall dark sketch of boyhood. Really, though, Fante depicts the community of boys in standard form, governed as it is by the socializing processes of family, school, church, and friends. What distinguishes the novel's depiction of boyhood is Arturo, a realist's antihero.

Arturo

The eldest son of Svevo and Maria, Arturo is a character with some pluck, but no luck. One 1939 reviewer described him as the "chief interpreter" of the novel,[9] though, as previously noted, Arturo does not command complete narrative authority. In 1993, Neil Gordon declared him the "achingly real, crazily lyrical Arturo Bandini, a child's voice speaking from the jailhouse of family" (Gordon, 24). As in all of Fante's novels, this hero acts out his impulses. For example, Arturo, frustrated by his father's abandonment and his family's hunger, kills a chicken out of anger, then, out of remorse, cannot bring himself to eat it, then eats it with gusto as the food inspires rapture (*Wait*, 57). Frequently self-defeating and damning, Arturo's strategies follow only the logic of emotion. One's perception of Arturo seesaws in the episode where Arturo steals his mother's black cameo (a first anniversary gift from Svevo) to give to his beloved, Rosa Pinelli, in what he hopes will be a grand gesture of his love (*Wait*, 143). His parents' presently schismed relationship and the Bandinis' overall poverty underscore the depravity of the theft itself. Rosa's apparent indifference to him makes the act seem not only very sad but very futile. On the last day before Christmas vacation, Arturo leaves the classroom to slip the present into Rosa's coat, which is hanging in the hallway. His anonymous delivery of the cameo suggests that Arturo knows that she will not want to receive such a gift from him. That night, en route to the Altar Boy Banquet (where he hopes to find Rosa grateful and pleasantly surprised by his proclamation of love) Arturo is felled by anxiety and fears he is having a heart attack: "it came to him like piercing daggers that this was God's warning, this was His way of letting him know that God knew his crime: he, the thief, filcher of his mother's cameo, sinner against the decalogue" (*Wait*, 153). Arturo, always taking things too far, continues his mental flagellation: "Thief, thief, outcast of God, hell's child with a black mark across the book of his soul" (*Wait*, 153). Straight to the confessional Arturo goes and there a kind priest, Father Andrew, advises how he can solve the moral predicament he has created for himself and receive absolution. So happy that all is right between him and God again, Arturo kneels in the church, and "[f]or two hours . . . he pray[s] every prayer he knew" (*Wait*, 155). Now at peace, he decides that when he returns home that night he will tell his mother the story and feels that she will forgive him. He leaves the church, and as he enters the banquet he sees Rosa, who is waiting for him. She asks to talk to him outside and he realizes "that something awful was about to happen" (*Wait*, 156). Rosa returns the cameo, saying: "I can't accept stolen property. My mother says you probably stole this" (*Wait*, 156). He insists that it is not stolen—a lie— which puts him back in the red as far as sin goes. Then, ever the gracious loser, he pushes Rosa into the snow. Compounding his misdeeds, he finally throws the cameo "with all his might" over the roof of a two-story house.

Arturo is misguided, vengeful, insecure, callous, hopeful, and cynical. He is also sympathetic because his intentions are usually kind. For example, during his mother's deep depression it is Arturo who cares for her and his brothers. But Arturo's good intentions are often derailed at any sign of conflict. Gordon remarks indirectly on these contending forces when he says that Arturo "speaks directly on the page, with an honesty so raw that it is better called vulnerability" (Gordon, 24). Arturo acts on his lesser instincts and feels acutely any insult to his pride. The same raw emotions and futile gestures that repulse also make Arturo Bandini imminently sympathetic.

Arturo dreams that his baseball stardom will be the antidote to the family's many shames: destitution, infidelities, the inability to pay the grocer. He also interprets baseball as the solution to his personal insecurity; his baseball dreams link very clearly to his desire to live the American dream. Baseball is, after all, the quintessence of American sports. During the winter, Arturo looks for any climatic encouragement to start playing again. In one corner of the school's baseball field he spies a spot "where the wind had banked the snow and thrown a dirty lace over it . . . it was dry enough otherwise, perfect weather for practice" (*Wait*, 230). He tries convincing the team to meet later for a workout, but he gets no takers: "Even Rodriquez, the catcher, the one kid in all the school who loved baseball as fanatically as himself" refused him with a quizzical look. "Wait," they tell him, "Wait until Spring, Bandini" (*Wait*, 230). And so the coaddressee of the book's title is left to ponder his pending glory. In the meantime, he rationalizes away the intimidating advantages of the town's wealthier children: "Wintertime, Christmas time, rich kid time: they had high top boots and bright mufflers and fur-lined gloves. But it didn't worry him much. His time was the Springtime. . . . Can't get to first base because you got a fancy necktie" (*Wait*, 133). Arturo awaits the democratic spring where one advances— where he advances—via talent and not wealth. For him, "Wintertime" is "rich kid time." Arturo and his ego must wait until the spring returns.

Svevo and Maria

Committed as *Wait Until Spring, Bandini* is to the story of Arturo, the drama of Svevo and Maria is also emphasized. Gerald Managan considers this book Fante's masterpiece and the portrait of Svevo and Maria its "most important achievement" (Managan, 303). Their fractured relationship should be considered the novel's main event.

One of the more important figures in most of Fante's fiction and especially in *Wait Until Spring, Bandini* is the strong, sometimes tyrannical, father. Bricklayer, stonemason, drinker, and gambler from Abruzzi, Italy, an undependable provider for his family, this character is a near constant in Fante's novels. Svevo Bandini is very much like Fante depicted his own father in letters to Mencken and friends. With a booming voice and perpetual histrionics, Svevo is expressive (both in his craft and his gesticulations), frequently overwhelmed by his emotions, and a medium-grade scoundrel. Between both personas—that of Fante's real father, Nick, and that of Svevo Bandini—parallels abound. Both men, for instance, abandoned their families for a time.

The first chapter of *Wait Until Spring, Bandini* is devoted almost wholly to Svevo. The snowy December night weighs on him as he returns home after losing at the poker table. He thinks about his debts to the grocer, to his friend Rocco Saccone, and to the banker who owns his house. Now a loser at cards on top of it all, Svevo is in a foul mood and his situation is dire. Nevertheless, the novel's first line establishes Svevo's spirited reaction to it: "He came along, kicking the deep snow. Here was a disgusted man" (*Wait*, 11). These two short declarative sentences—one of Fante's prose trademarks—establish two defining elements of Svevo Bandini's temperament and character: angry and in motion. There is an element of the ridiculous in Svevo too. That he expresses his disgust by kicking snow gives the reader an indication that he is actually laughable. A 1938 review of the book charging that Svevo "expresses his bitterness with infantile abandon" is not completely unfair (De Kay, 7). But we are quickly led to look further than the farcical aspects of Svevo's temper. Good reasons exist for this man's acrimony: "He was cold and there were holes in his shoes. That morning he had patched the holes on the inside with pieces of cardboard from a maca-roni box. The macaroni in that box was not paid for. He had thought of that as he placed the cardboard inside of his shoes" (Wait, 11). Svevo's poverty puts him at the mercy of the cold.

But Svevo is not simply a man without volition, an object upon which an environment of poverty acts. Svevo himself acts, making choices within his circumstances, though the parade of these poor deci-sions forces the reader to question his wisdom. His own cognizance of his poor decisions makes this ironic. For example, Svevo is aware of the absurdity that a man who grew up in Italy's mountains, hating the snow there because it prevented work, would move halfway around the world to Colorado and find himself in the same environment: "It harassed him always, that beautiful snow. He could never understand why he didn't go to California. Yet he stayed in Colorado, in the deep snow, because it was too late now" (Wait, 12). This passage begs the question not answered in the novel—not why he does not move to California, for surely he is too poor for such a journey, but why did he go to Colorado in the first place? Svevo lives in a place where not only is he unemployed half the year but his family is also outcast. This unexplained life empha-sizes Svevo's chaotic nature.

Svevo lives in a world of materiality. His profession is of the most concrete kind: he builds structures with stone and brick. When he is working on Effie Hildegarde's rental property, he takes pride in the physical durability of his creations: "This, he vowed, would be one of the finest little bricklaying jobs in the state of Colorado. Fifty years from now, a hundred years from now, two hundred, the fireplace would still be standing" (Wait, 188–89). Also solid and durable is Svevo's body; he is "all muscles" (Wait, 12). His physicality is the outward symbol of his personality; his body is the eloquent expression of his personality, partic-ularly when he is angry. When he slips on Arturo's sled while walking up the front walkway, his anger unleashes: "He had told that boy, that little bastard, to keep his sled out of the front walk . . . [he] felt the snow's cold attacking his hands like frantic ants. He got to his feet, raised his eyes to the sky, shook his fist at God, and nearly collapsed with fury" (*Wait*, 15). Cursing God, cursing Arturo, he proceeds with "systematic fiendishness" to destroy the sled. Only when he has finished doing so does he remember that the sled cost seven dollars and fifty cents: "Seven dollars and fifty cents torn to pieces. *Diavolo!* Let the boy buy another sled. He preferred a new one anyway" (*Wait*, 15). In this energetic scene Svevo displaces the responsibility for his act. He destroyed the sled, but, he reasons, the boy wanted a new one anyway. Throughout the novel when Svevo is angry, he is violent to inanimate objects. In another scene he becomes impatient with the shoelaces his cold hands will not let him untie. Though Maria tries to stop him, he rips them to get out of his boots (17). Later in the novel he takes on some tape he is using to bandage a wound: " 'Don't get tough with *me!*' he said to the tape." And then he "growled: 'No piece of tape can get the best of Svevo Bandini' " (*Wait*, 210).

Svevo's physicality is expressed through creative, not just destructive forms. Needing a channel for his unemployed energy, each winter morning Svevo "shovel[s] every clod of snow from every path in and around the yard, half a block down the street, under the clothes lines, far down the alley, piling it high, moving it around, cutting it viciously with his flat shovel" (*Wait*, 26). The narrator describes Maria watching Svevo from her kitchen window; she can see her husband on the other side of the fence, "his shovel peering over the top now and then, throwing puffs of snow back to the sky" (*Wait*, 26). His industriousness is futile, and as he throws "puffs of snow back to the sky" his inability to conquer his circumstances seems total. But when working, Svevo is a shining example of refinement: "Peeling off his coat, he plunged to the task . . . He sang as he worked, a song of Spring: *Come Back to Sorrento*. The empty house sighed with echo, the cold rooms filling with the ring of his voice, the crack of his hammer and the plink of his trowel. Gala day: the time passed quickly. The room grew warm with the heat of his energy, the window panes wept for joy as the frost melted and the street became visible" (*Wait*, 188–89). All of Svevo's energy, unchecked elsewhere in the novel, is tamed and channeled while he works. Up early, he works hard and with careful craftsmanship. The narrator describes this aspect of Svevo when he repairs Effie Hildegarde's fireplace: "He had done a careful job: not a speck of mortar smeared the faces of the brick he had laid. Even the canvas was clean" (*Wait*, 178).

Sometimes compelling, sometimes repellent, Svevo Bandini always dominates the scene. Still, he is not a monster. In chapter 8 Svevo's long apostrophe to Maria begins where he imagines justifying to her, and himself, the affair with the "Widow Hildegarde" (*Wait,* 171). His address to the absent Maria begins: "It was like this, Maria: ten days ago your mother wrote that letter, and I got mad and left the house, because I can't stand the woman. I must go away when she comes. And so I went away. I got lots of troubles, Maria. The kids. The house. The snow . . . And I'm worried, and your mother is coming, and I say to myself, I say, I think I'll go downtown and have a few drinks. Because I got troubles. Because I got kids. Ah, Maria" (*Wait,* 171). When the narrator then takes back the point of view, the perspective switches from Svevo's first person to the third person: "He had gone downtown to the Imperial Poolhall" (*Wait,* 171). Even within the third-person point of view, we see the narrative absorbed by Svevo. He confesses to insecurities in his monologue that are difficult to imagine him communicating to his family. He explains: "There are things a man cannot tell his wife. Would Maria understand that surge of humility as he crossed the handsome room, the embarrassment as he staggered when his worn shoes, wet with snow, failed to grip the shining yellow floor? Could he tell Maria that the attractive woman felt a sudden pity for him?" (*Wait,* 175). Svevo's deep relief upon being employed demonstrates how desperately he has wanted to work. After his first day working at Effie Hildegarde's house he "slept well: no falling into black bottomless pits, no green-eyed serpents slithering after him through his dreams" (*Wait,* 191). The employment Effie offers him soothes his deepest anxieties.

In conversations with the widow it becomes quickly apparent that she and Svevo have little in common. Effie's education and wealth give her access to worlds from which he is kept; even his homeland seems to be less in his possession than hers: "So he was an Italian? Splendid. Only last year she had traveled in Italy. Beautiful. He must be so proud of his heritage. Did he know that the cradle of western civilization was Italy? Had he ever seen the Campo Santo, the Cathedral of St. Peter's, the paintings of Michelangelo, the blue Mediterranean? The Italian Riviera?" (*Wait,* 176). Svevo responds to her quizzing with humility and explains why he has not seen what she has of Italy: "No, he had seen none of these. In simple words he told her that he was from Abruzzi, that he had never been that far North, never to Rome. He had worked hard as a boy. There had been no time for anything else" (*Wait,* 176). The widow alights on the mention of his region of Italy. "Abruzzi! The Widow knew everything. Then surely he had read the works of D'Annunzio—he, too, was an Abruzzian" (*Wait,* 177). As Svevo and

Effie talk it is clear that conversation, though a ritual of their affair, is better dispensed with. Their articulated experiences are separated by the almost unbridgeable gulf of their socioeconomic class.

Svevo is so highly conscious of these disparities that when Effie indicates her sexual interest in him, he does not believe it: "He could not be sure of himself. He squinted his eyes as he watched her. No—she could not mean it. This woman had too much money . . . What he had been thinking had best be forgotten" (*Wait*, 198). When he does not respond to her overtures, she taunts him by smiling: "You fool." Svevo "grins his confusion" and turn and walks down the hall to the front door. When she insults him—"You fool! You ignorant peasant"—Svevo understands the sexual scenario she desires that figures him as the lusty peasant and she as the victim of his savage prowess. The narrator portrays Svevo's version of the interlude by making clear that Effie cries with "ecstatic pain . . . her weeping a pretense, a beseechment for mercilessness" (*Wait*, 199). Her submission, pretended or otherwise, fills the once insecure Svevo with a sense of undistilled mastery. The narrator describes the violent sexual union between these characters: "she was struggling to tear herself away. She winced in terrible joy as he stepped back, her ripped blouse streaming from his two fists" (*Wait*, 198); "each gasp [of hers] his victory" (*Wait*, 199). The violence described is alleviated somewhat by the mitigating half of the oxymorons used, such as "terrible *joy*," "*ecstatic* pain," "*delicious* torment" (italics added). The following sentence from this scene is both unnerving and confusing: "He could have done away with her had he desired, reduced her scream to a whisper, but he arose and walked into the room where the fireplace glowed lazily in the quick Winter darkness, leaving her weeping and choking on the bed" (*Wait*, 199). The brutally straightforward passage puzzles since the expression "done away with her" customarily entails murder. Did Svevo consider killing Effie Hildegarde? Another reading of "he could have done away with her" is that Svevo left Effie sexually unfinished, to coin a phrase. Since she follows him to the living room and "fell on her knees before him" is the reader to conclude that she is begging Svevo for sexual completion? What she begs for is left unclear. In any case, their relationship continues like this for days: its pattern of uncomfortable conversation leading unvaryingly to sex.

In Svevo's relationship with Effie many aspects of his identity—his notion of himself as a craftsman who deserves praise, his masculine physicality, his sexuality—are amplified and, ultimately, perhaps ironically, self-destruct. Ironically, that is, because in this relationship Svevo's masculinity is both accentuated and sabotaged. On the one hand, he is more physical and physically powerful than she is, and Effie dramatizes that disparity when she makes her play for him. On the other hand, once Svevo has conquered her in bed, the buying power that her wealth permits her ensures that she has power over him. He becomes, in effect, a kept man. She buys him extravagant gifts that he could never match: fine cigars, liquor, and a pair of kangaroo leather shoes (*Wait*, 195–202). In one scene Arturo journeys up to Effie's house to check on his absent father. Arturo witnesses his father stepping out onto the porch to take in the night air and smoke a cigar: Svevo "wore bright red bedroom slippers, blue pajamas, and a red lounging robe that had white tassels on the sash ends. Holy Jumping Jiminy, he looked like Helmer the banker and President Roosevelt. . . . O boy, what a man!" (*Wait*, 237). Though the boy is impressed with his father's improved apparel, the narrator gives a portrait of a dandy. Effie feeds, employs, and clothes Svevo.

Svevo and Effie's relationship is overtly predicated not on the exchange of power but on the lending of power. For a time, Svevo dominates the bedroom and Effie dominates the rest, but the wealth that she bestows on him does not endure. Effie pays him more than a hundred dollars on Christmas Eve for his work and, perhaps, for other services rendered. Svevo, returning after days away, comes home with the money and tells his family he won it playing cards: "Pretty good card-player, Papa" (*Wait*, 161). His wife is not fooled by the lie and knows the source of the cash. After clawing Svevo's face, Maria burns the money in the fireplace since to her it symbolizes his transgression. With the money reduced to ashes, Svevo, in effect, makes nothing from two weeks of work. Finally, when Svevo leaves Effie at the end of the book, he simply walks away from the house, and one must surmise he is not paid for the walls and benches he built after his Christmas Eve return. So, actually, Svevo makes no money at all. That Svevo cannot make money from the town's wealthiest and most extravagant resident is, in some ways, absurd and certainly in keeping with Svevo's string of bad choices and bad luck. Svevo ends the affair just as poor as when he began it. The trespass exists in memory only; no material symbol remains.

Svevo is at his most appealing when we see evidence of his unhappiness at being estranged from his family. When Arturo goes to tell Svevo that Maria wants him at home, Svevo is dressing stones on Effie's property, shaping them to fit a stone bench. Upon hearing that Maria is no longer angry, he places a stone and then stands over it, "breathing hard.

His hand went to his eye, the finger brushing away a trickle at the side of his nose. 'Something in my eye,' he said. 'A little piece of stone.'" The intuitive Arturo responds to his father's tears with diplomacy: "I know. I've had them." (*Wait,* 260). Svevo has been wanting to go home and (mentally) he welcomes his son's invitation to return. Perhaps drawing the focus back to Fante the man, we see in Svevo's scripted rationalization an apologia that a literary son wrote for his own errant father.

In contradistinction to her husband, Maria is evanescent, a woman whose spiritual world almost supplants her earthly one. Her days are spent tending to the house and praying for the souls of her husband and sons, hoping that somewhere someone is praying for her. One critic calls her "Christ-struck,"[10] but the more accurate, if less zingy, description must be "Mary-struck," since it is to the Virgin Mary that her prayers are directed. Fred Gadarphé describes an emphasis on the Virgin Mary as part of the Mediterranean Catholic tradition present in Italian American fiction (Gadarphé, 61). This Marianist tradition dominates Maria's landscape; she even identifies herself with the Virgin: "her name was Maria, and so was the Savior's mother, and she had gone to that other Maria over miles and miles of rosary beads" (*Wait,* 32). Though the earthly Svevo thinks of his wife in less magisterial terms—as a ghost and a "religious fanatic" (*Wait,* 22)—the narrator reverently describes Maria at her rosary:

> She had no need in her heart for either book or magazine. She had her own way of escape, her own passage into contentment: her rosary. That string of white beads, the tiny links worn in a dozen places and held together by strands of white thread which in turn broke regularly, was, bead for bead, her quiet flight out of the world. Hail Mary, full of grace, the Lord is with thee. And Maria began to climb. Bead for bead, life and living fell away. Hail Mary, Hail Mary. Dream without sleep encompassed her. Passion without flesh lulled her. Love without death crooned the melody of belief. She was away: she was free; she was no longer Maria, American or Italian, poor or rich, with or without electric washing machines and vacuum cleaners; here was the land of all-possessing. Hail Mary, Hail Mary, over and over, a thousand and a hundred thousand times, prayer upon prayer, the sleep of the body, the escape of the mind, the death of memory, the slipping away of pain, the deep silent reverie of belief. Hail Mary and Hail Mary. It was for this that she lived. (*Wait,* 75)

The rosary mentally delivers Maria from her desperate straits, her erratic husband; in short, from her many worldly cares. The narrator's depiction of prayer as an "escape" could imply a certain derision—as if her quest and hopes were bankrupt or at least deluded. Nevertheless, Maria's religiousness plays a crucial role in the novel. At the end of the first chapter Maria's faith in her husband wavers. Svevo has left home to avoid seeing his mother-in-law. Maria is unhappy with his absence but does not feel her marriage threatened, at first. Then doubt materializes: "She could trust Svevo. He would float his brains on a sea of whiskey, but he would not be unfaithful to her. She knew that. But could she?" (*Wait*, 45). That small question that occurs to her—"could she?"—must seem to her a serious breach since she reacts dramatically: "With a gasp she threw herself into the chair by the table and wept as she buried her face in her hands" (*Wait*, 45). Maria's lost faith in her husband precedes his infidelity. A causal link between the abstract act (loss of faith) and the physical act (adultery) is suggested by the novel's events; the instrumentality of Maria's loss of faith is evident.

Her otherworldly presence, however, does not exclude Maria from terra firma. To read her as simply a specter of Catholicism glosses over the intricacies of her character. Described as naive and innocent, she is remarkable for being actually more attuned to the world that surrounds her than her doubting son and husband. For instance, she is prophetic: after making love with her husband she can gauge to the dollar how much Svevo lost gambling (*Wait*, 25), and she knows when Svevo has broken their marriage vows. She also knows, even before Arturo confesses to it, that he has stolen 10 cents from her purse.

> "Mamma," he groped. "I did something."
> "It's alright," she said. "I knew."
> That surprised him. How could she have possibly known? He had swiped that dime with consummate perfection. He had fooled her. . . .
> (*Wait*, 83)

Of course, Arturo had not fooled her. His realization that her powers of prophecy are stronger than his at deceit unnerves him.

Maria also works wonders in the everyday sphere. The stove, for instance, cooperates with no one but her (*Wait*, 28). In chapter 4 her abilities to perform in the human sphere are tested when she has to ask the grocer for more food on credit. Though her skills are awkward in this exchange, her tenacity means that she can keep feeding her family long after the family is broke, an ability that the worldly Svevo lacks.

Another worldly aspect of Maria is the strength of her own sexuality. Critics are apt to reduce the Bandinis to their differences alone; one reviewer in 1939, for instance, described them simply: Svevo as a "lusty father" and Maria as a "religious mother" (Walton, 72). In terms of sexual drive, though, Maria rivals Svevo. She is portrayed as a woman "who had only to think of the muscle in [Svevo's] loins and her body and mind melted like the spring snows" (*Wait*, 12–13). From the first chapter the Bandinis are portrayed as passionately involved with each other: "Her name was Maria, and she was so patient, waiting for him, touching the muscle at his loins, so patient, kissing him here and there, and then the great heat he loved consumed him and she lay back. 'Ah, Svevo. So wonderful!' " (*Wait*, 24). The postcoital passage goes on, and we see that they are not exactly in love with each other, but that both Svevo and Maria are in love with Svevo: "He loved her with such gentle fierceness, so proud of himself, thinking all the time: she is not so foolish, this Maria, she knows what is good" (*Wait*, 24). Sometimes Svevo thinks of her desire for him and is overwhelmed by it, as when he envisions her "endlessly waiting for passion" (*Wait*, 14). Later, the pull of her desire for her husband distracts her from her rosary when she is sitting in her darkened living room, praying and watching men walk down the sidewalk: "In the street a man smoking a pipe walked by. . . . She compared him with Bandini; he was taller, but he had none of Svevo's gusto in his step. . . . Another man passed in the street. . . . Svevo was a much finer looking man than he. . . . But these were distractions. It was sacrilegious to allow stray thoughts to interfere with prayer" (*Wait*, 85). For the Bandinis, sex fuses their corporeal and evanescent selves. In the union of Svevo and Maria, Fante ably depicts the ecstasy that transports the physical body into the spiritual world.

Ethnicity

The Bandini family members comprise an amalgam of ethnic identifications and allegiances. Though born and raised in the United States, Maria is the most heavily invested in the Italian peasant tradition. In fact, Maria is less adapted to life in the United States than her Italian-born husband. Maria irritates Svevo by referring to "American women" in a way that signals she does not include herself in the American species (*Wait*, 73). Svevo takes pride in his Italian heritage, yet "now that he had citizenship papers, never regarded himself as an Italian" (*Wait*, 74). Arturo, however, sees his father as thoroughly Italian. After a family argument at the breakfast table, Arturo thinks: "What kind of people were these Wops? Look at his father, there . . . Oh sure, he was a Dago Wop, so he had to have a mustache . . . Oh God, these Italians!" (*Wait*, 37). Being Italian is less distasteful to Arturo after he falls for Rosa Pinelli; in that case, he hopes that their mutual Italian background will unite them.

Arturo mediates between his parents' complicated sense of ethnicity and in many other ways as well. He is a compound of their characters: his father's corporeality is leavened in Arturo by the influence of his mother's spirituality (Arturo, after all, prophesies Rosa's death). His mother's religiosity is complicated by his father's secularism; that dual influence leaves Arturo a religious skeptic: that is, a skeptic who is also religious. This aspect is readily seen when Arturo worries about his soul and his sins (*Wait*, 111–13). Arturo also runs interference between his parents while they are estranged. Though unlucky in love himself, he brings Svevo and Maria back together at the novel's end.

When it was first published, *Wait Until Spring, Bandini* scored respectable successes. Not long after the book came out, it was published in London by Routledge (*Letters*, 151). Soon after that, a writer optioned the book to write a play for the New York stage (*Letters*, 154). For a time Southern California actor and Californio gadfly Leo Carrillo was slated to play the part of Svevo (*Letters*, 157). Ultimately, *Wait Until Spring, Bandini* never made it to the stage. But in 1989, over 50 years after the novel was first published, and soon after the novel's 1983 republication by Black Sparrow Press, *Wait Until Spring, Bandini* made it to the screen (Spotnitz, 40–44, 54). Reflecting Fante's international popularity in the United States and in Europe, it was directed by the Belgian Dominique Deruddere and produced by organizations based in Belgium, Italy, America, and France. Zoetrope, the production company of U.S. director and cineaste Francis Ford Coppola,[11] was among the producers. The movie starred Faye Dunaway, Joe Mantegna, and Italian actress Ornella Muti. Though the film did capture the energy of Fante's work, Tom Christie calls it "disappointing to say the least."[12] The cinematography shows a lovely mountain town and does a good job of staying true to the book's depiction of Rocklin. What the film does not accomplish is the complexity of the characters: in the book these individuals have time to develop, while film, by its nature, cannot capture the subtle contradictions in Fante's narrative.

Wait Until Spring, Bandini remains one of Fante's best-selling and acclaimed novels.

1933 Was a Bad Year

1933 Was a Bad Year's posthumous discovery was nothing short of amazing because no one knew it existed. It was a psychic who instructed a family member to go back to Fante's files (which had already been carefully examined) to look for another manuscript.[13] We know Fante started the book in the early 1950s as he made passing reference to the novel's contents in a 1954 letter to a publisher he was trying to interest in another book he was working on, what later became *The Brotherhood of the Grape (Letters*, 231). Probably Fante wrote the remainder of *1933 Was a Bad Year* sometime later in the 1950s or 1960s, but the material never made it to print during Fante's lifetime (*Letters*, 231). Joyce Fante postulates that Fante sent to publishers what he considered the first half of *1933 Was a Bad Year*, but when he received no interest in it, he was too discouraged to complete the book's second half (Gollard, 13). This circumstance may be a happy accident, since the book feels complete as it is.

One frustration for Fante may have been that *1933 Was a Bad Year* retraces the material he had already utilized both in many short stories and in *Wait Until Spring, Bandini*. Though the characters' names are different, *1933 Was a Bad Year*, in many ways, extends the plot trajectory begun in *Wait Until Spring, Bandini*. The conflicts are identical: ethnic marginalization, poverty, a father's infidelity, a savage Italian grandmother, hopeless and unrequited love, an evolving identity in perpetual crisis, guilt, God, and baseball. The most significant difference between the novels lies in the older age of the protagonist: in the later novel Dominic Molise is 17, about to graduate from high school. To call *1933 Was a Bad Year* a simple reworking of the material of *Wait Until Spring, Bandini* would not be unfair but it would be shortsighted. Of the two novels set in Fante's childhood Colorado, *1933 Was a Bad Year* is the tighter, more accomplished book; a review in the *New Yorker* enthused that it is a "stunning short novel."[14]

Dominic Molise narrates *1933 Was a Bad Year*, telling the story of his life during the winter of 1933 from the vantage of many years later. This memoir style is indicated in a few signaling phrases such as "in those days," which is said twice in the novel's first chapter (*Year*, 8–9). Like *Wait Until Spring, Bandini*, the novel opens with a character walking home in the snow, but this time that character is the teenage Dominic Molise. As he walks, he thinks himself into a metaphysical quandary: "Look, I said, for in those days I was a believer who spoke frankly to his God: Lord, what gives?" (*Year,* 8). Dominic wonders about death and life, why he was born into such a poor family, and why he was born at all. But his confidence in his athletic talent soon overpowers his existential crisis. What could be more powerful than an existential crisis? A belief in one's pitching prowess: "The Arm kept me going, that sweet left arm . . . my blessed, holy arm that came from God, and if The Lord created me out of a poor bricklayer he hung me with jewels when he hinged that whizzer to my collarbone" (*Year,* 9). Dom reveres his arm, which he capitalizes and gives its own article: "The Arm." He keeps The Arm "soaked with Sloan's Liniment . . . I reeked with it, sometimes sent out of class to wash the pine tartness away, but I walked out proudly without shame, conscious of my destiny, steeled against the sneers of the boys and the tilted nostrils of the girls" (*Year,* 9). His pitching ability is confirmed by school kids who talk to Dom about games he has won. Though the reader is aware that a great pitcher in a small town is not necessarily major league caliber, Dom's self-confidence enables him to brave the obstacles of his poverty, his luckless love life, and his difficult family.

Dominic lives in a "crowded house" (*Year,* 14) with his two brothers, sister, mother, father, and vituperative paternal grandmother, Bettina. Bettina, who resides in a tiny corner room off the kitchen, is "a small fierce old lady . . . the skin at her temples so pale and transparent you could almost see inside her head" (*Year,* 16). There really is no need to see inside Grandma Bettina's head since she says exactly what she thinks and hides nothing. When Dom is in the kitchen doing his homework, Grandma Bettina, the "deadly enemy of the light company," addresses him: "There he sits . . . The brilliant young American, the product of an American womb, the pride of his dim-witted mother, the hope of the coming generation, there he sits, burning electricity" (*Year,* 16).[15]

With an immigrant stonemason father who has not worked in five months and a religious mother more Italian peasant than American (though she is U.S. born), the 17-year-old Dominic feels impeded by his situation. There is further conflict pending; with his high school graduation only months away, the question of Dominic's profession needs to be answered soon. While Dom believes in his baseball talent, his father insists he pursue the Molise legacy of bricklaying: "This June you graduate. Then we'll go to work. We'll show them! Show the whole world. Father and son. We'll pay our debts, save our money" (*Year,* 31). Though Dominic dreams of baseball fame, when his father overcomes his customary pride to admit, "We're in trouble. . . . We owe everybody—the

rent, the lights, the gas, the butcher, the doctor, the bank, the lumber
yard" (*Year,* 30), Dom pities his father and sets his hopes aside to lay
bricks for the survival of his family. That Dom does not think that the
circumstances of his family or his father's fortune can ever improve
makes his agreeing to be a bricklayer touching. Dom feels his father
"would go on working year after year until his strength gave out, until
he could stoop no more over a wall, and the trowel fell from his hand"
(*Year,* 30). Into this fatalistic prognosis, Dom gloomily inserts himself.
He imagines his acquiescence to his father to be the right decision, but
one that dooms him: "So there it was. The whole book. The Tragic Life
of Dominic Molise, written by his father. Part One: The Thrills of Bricklaying. Part Two: Fun in a Lumber Yard. Part Three: How to Let Your
Father Ruin Your Life. Part Four: Here Lies Dominic Molise, Obedient
Son" (*Year,* 31). In spite of the young man's resignation to his fate, the
contest for Dom's future is not settled in the first chapter, or even by the
book's end.

Opposed to his father's belief that he should be a bricklayer are not
only Dom's own dreams for his pitching arm but those of others. The
next day at school, after a morning meditating in Church (he had had a
vision of the Virgin Mary in his bedroom the night before—she looked
like Carole Lombard), Dom strolls into the schoolyard where lunchtime
socializing is in full swing. A couple of freshmen pay their respects by
asking about The Arm and the overall state of the St. Catherine's team:

> "Hey, ain't you Dominic Molise?"
> "Righto."
> It was like being interviewed by a couple of sports writers.
> "I saw you pitch against Boulder Prep," he said. "Man, were you hot!"
> I smiled modestly. "A two-hitter, if memory serves."
> "You struck out nineteen."
> "One of my better days." (*Year,* 43)

The reverence these two boys show to Dom's arm serves to remove
doubts the reader might have regarding a memoirist's inflated estima-
tion of his talents. It also demonstrates the cocky self-assurance that
buoys Dom through upcoming humiliations.

After Dom himself, The Arm's biggest booster is Dominic's best
friend Kenny Parrish. Dom and Kenny spend their winter afternoons
playing catch in the Elks Club basement, a club in which Kenny's very
wealthy father is a member. When Dom tells his friend that his father
has extracted a promise to abandon baseball for bricklaying, Kenny is

outraged ("Over my dead body!" [*Year,* 55]). Kenny, himself fed up with the snow, suggests they leave town, travel to the Cubs spring training camp at Catalina Island in California, and try out for the team.[16] He assures Dom that his are the "fingers of an artist . . . Just as precious as Yehudi Menuhin's. When I think of them laying brick it makes my blood run cold" (*Year,* 60). With all the passionate conviction of youth, Dom swears he will never pick up a trowel and agrees to the trip: "Let's go, Kenny! Let's get the hell out of here before we die!" (*Year,* 61). When Kenny figures it will cost them $50 apiece, Dom burns when he remembers how desperately poor his family is in comparison to Kenny's family: "All the furniture in our house, including the kitchen stove, wasn't worth that . . . We were so broke that even the poor nuns at St. Catherine's accepted us tuition free" (*Year,* 61–62). He perceives Kenny to be "talking of fifty dollars as if it was fifty cents" and lashes out at him: "Screw you, and your big-assed mother and your grouchy old man, and your big house and your servants and your cars and your money" (*Year,* 62). They are friends again before long, but the friction over their economic disparities reemerges throughout the novel; Dom and Kenny share an ambition for baseball stardom, but only one can afford the bus ticket.

Something else unattainable to Dominic but urgently desired is the attention of Kenny's older sister, Dorothy. A beautiful psychology major at the university, she barely notices Dom when he comes around the house. Dorothy and Dom share neither interests nor backgrounds. Dom notes the differences in their education when he looks at the shelves of books she reads and off-handedly comments that they are, perhaps, showy: "They were mostly new books, the kind displayed in the front window of Martin's Stationery Store: Hemingway, Caldwell, Bromfield, Waugh. My own reading range was strictly St. Catherine style: *Quo Vadis, Life of St. Teresa, Ivanhoe, The Deerslayer, Two Years before the Mast*" (*Year,* 51).

The first time Dom sees Dorothy is at the Parrishes' hardware store; Dom, in fact, sees quite a bit of her when she climbs a ladder to get an item for him. Holding the ladder for Dorothy, Dom is transfixed by her, a "tawny cloud floating in the tent of her skirt" (*Year,* 48). When she catches his stare, his shame and panic send him crashing out the door. Three years later Dom sees her again at the Parrish house, and he is relieved that she does not recognize him. Later he makes a play for Dorothy by feigning a desire to be psychoanalyzed. Her college girl's grasp of psychoanalysis is vulgar Freud: all mothers and fathers and toilet training (*Year*, 85 –88). Dorothy and Dom share coffee and scrambled eggs in the Parrish kitchen while she asks him questions. In the midst of her analysis, he confesses his love: "I stood up without feet and found myself pulled toward her, falling to my knees before her, my arms around her hips, my face in the depths of her dress, and the demon had me totally in his power" (*Year*, 88). Not surprisingly, Dorothy fights his advance. After his kamikaze seduction fails, Dorothy drops out of the book, soon forgotten.

Peter Molise, Dom's father, spends all his time at the Onyx poolhall, hustling pool. Peter is "far and away the best billiard player in Roper, but his skill went against him because it was hard to lure competitors, and he had to give away too many points" (*Year*, 21). Peter is also a master bricklayer, but the weather conspires against him and most of the year it is too cold to lay bricks because of the frozen mortar. Master of two arts, bricklaying and pool playing, he does not, or cannot, succeed at either. His wife, Mary, correctly surmises that Peter is not being faithful to her, but the woman he has taken up with is of an unexpected variety. One night Dom goes to find his father—ostensibly to discuss again his baseball dreams. He is directed by an acquaintance to Edna Pruitt's house. The sign outside reads:

Edna Mae Pruitt, DSC, PHM
Chiropractic Masseuse
Personalized Manipulation
Spiritual Healing
Day or Night. Phone 37W (96)

Dom looks inside the house and beholds as quiet and staid a love affair as could be imagined: "It was just two people, Papa and Edna Pruitt, sitting quietly in the parlor, under a big picture of President Hoover. Edna was in a rocking chair, knitting a sock, and my father sat at a bridge table playing solitaire" (*Year*, 97). It is an affair that surprises more than shocks Dom. In the beginning chapter of the novel when Peter has come home from the poolhall covered in lipstick, Dom feels strongly the betrayal of his mother this lipstick trace represents. The later, more intriguing scene of *a*sexual adultery with Edna Pruitt is brief. Perhaps the spiritual healing that her sign advertises as one of her skills is responsible for the "strange serenity" (*Year*, 97) Dom has never seen on his father's face before.

Glimpsing his father in this new and interesting light gives Dom the courage to lobby once again for his own destiny. Dom and Peter are walking home on a dark snowy night. Dom lobbies his cause by using the examples of other Italian American baseball players—Joe DiMaggio, Babe Pinelli, Frank Crosetti, Lou Fonseca—to convince his father of the verity of his dream (*Year*, 98). When he tells his father he wants to go to California to try out for the Cubs, and it is clear how desperately Dom believes in his talent, Peter's stubbornness yields a bit: "Pain and sadness softened his face. He put his hand on my shoulder, hesitant to speak what was on his mind" (*Year*, 99). Peter's concern is that Dom is not tough enough: "Those men are like iron. They're hard, tough. They'll grind you in the dirt. They'll break your heart" (*Year*, 99). Though Dom thinks that his father's foreignness prevents understanding, a dream to succeed elsewhere would be very familiar to Peter. The reader infers the scene must be similar to the one played out between Peter and his own father when he decided to come to the United States.[17] To talk of the broken heart he foresees for his own son suggests that Peter too must have once believed in the feasibility of his own success, must have once been sure that his talent would carry the day and ensure his fortune. As he and his son walk they pass examples of Peter's talent: "All over town you could see his handiwork—schools, churches, homes, garages, chimneys, driveways, terraces, fireplaces, sidewalks of stone, of concrete, of brick, steps going up and steps going down" (*Year*, 101). But naturally, Dom cannot recognize the similarities between his situation and his father's: "Poor old Papa. What a life! But not Dom Molise. I had a way out, a gift of God, The Arm" (*Year*, 101). Though his father does not endorse his plan, neither does he forbid it and Dom feels he has won his point. Now his major worry is what it was originally: the $50 for the trip to California.

Dom decides to steal his father's concrete mixer—currently dormant in the shed, waiting for sunshine and work—and sell it to buy his passage to California. He tells himself it is only borrowing, not stealing, since in a couple of months, after signing a contract with the Cubs, he would "be able to buy [Peter] a brand new mixer, one of those super jobs" (*Year*, 105). Kenny opposes the idea, but he agrees to borrow his father's truck to help tow the mixer to sell at a building supply store out of town. Dom and Kenny are already in the alley with the mixer hooked up to the truck when the indomitable Grandma Bettina trudges through the snow behind the house to accost them, in flagrante delicto: " 'So this is the American way,' she said. 'To kill the soul of a man, and then chop off his hands. What will my son do without this machine? Do you expect him to mix mortar with a hoe?' " (*Year*, 112). Kenny, profoundly ashamed, abandons the truck and the crime scene altogether. Dom himself drives the truck away from his grandmother's castigations: "Looking straight ahead, I heard her speak of first and last things, of birth and death, of crime and damnation, of Judas and the fall of honor among sons" (*Year,* 113).

To avoid the notice of people who would recognize his father's mixer, Dom takes a back road out of town. The road leads through the cemetery where his grandfather, Giovanni Molise, is buried. Marking the grave is "the granite cross on the stone pedestal . . . as tall as a man and very slender, cloaked with snow, as if it wore a white shawl. The monument was my father's pride and joy. Off and on for two years he had worked on it in our shed, reducing a huge chunk of marble into the graceful cross, chipping and polishing the stone until it was as smooth as human skin" (*Year,* 114). At this tangible symbol of his father's love for his own father, Dom realizes that he cannot sell out his father's livelihood. He turns the truck back toward home.

Waiting for him there is a furious Peter Molise. Dominic tries to talk his way out of his near-crime, but Peter wants to fight: "If you can steal from me, you can fight me. Come on, hit me!" (*Year,* 117). Peter bloodies his son's nose and immediately is horrified at doing so. With handfuls of snow held to stop the bleeding, Dom again tells his father of his "hopes and despairs, the boredom of poverty," and of his desire for "the chance to leave home and try [his] hand at pro ball" (*Year,* 118). Recognizing his son's conviction, and perhaps wanting to experience again the thrill of gambling on an immigrant's dreams, Peter promises to help Dom. He returns from the poolhall later with $25, a huge sum of money for Peter, but still only a dollar more than a one-way ticket to California. Dom goes to tell Kenny to pack, but Mr. Parrish meets Dom at the door: "I want you to stay away from my son. . . . You're not welcome here. . . . Kenny's not going on this stupid junket. . . . Stay away from here, clear away on your side of town, or I'll call the police" (*Year,* 124–5). A discouraged Dom decides that he cannot make the trip without Kenny. In fact, Kenny seems to represent to Dom a kind of Anglo fetish, without which he cannot easily envision success: "I was too stupid to make it alone, I might go the wrong way, end up in Torricella Peligna, where I belonged" (*Year,* 125). Without Kenny, Dom fears he will revert to the feral state of his ancestors: Italy.

Walking back to his side of town, resigned to postponing his exodus, Dom is shocked to see his father's concrete mixer at Art's Service Station. It is dismantled with the "parts spread on the floor, the carburetor soaking in a bucket of gasoline" (*Year,* 126). Now it is Dom's turn to be horrified. Peter did not win the $25 playing pool, as Dom had assumed, but by a different kind of gambling, staking his son by selling the mixer himself. This effectively pins the livelihood of the entire family on Dom. When Art refuses to sell the mixer back, Dom is devastated. The book's final scene presents a desperate but enlightened son: "I put my arms around [the mixer] and kissed it with my mouth and cried for my father and all fathers, and sons too, for being alive in that time, for myself, because I had to go to California now, I had no choice, I had to make good" (*Year,* 127). Whether or not Fante meant to write a second half to the book, this scene is a fascinating place for the story to end. All the book's action leads up to a journey that the reader never sees. With Dom stripped of his sidekick and never witnessed traveling, *1933 Was a Bad Year* is an antipicaresque novel.

Dominic, Baseball, Authorship

That Fante did not make *1933 Was a Bad Year* an installment of the Bandini saga is curious. The protagonist's age (17) bridges that of the Arturo Bandinis of *Wait Until Spring, Bandini* (14) and *Ask the Dust* (20). All are from small town Colorado, the sons of Italian immigrant bricklaying fathers, religious mothers, and parochial school educations. All are characterized by passionate natures, strongly vacillating insecurity and confidence in themselves, and a fierce desire to conquer their inherited poverty. In fact, the elemental differences between *1933 Was a Bad Year* and the Bandini books are superficial and limited to family composition (there is a sister in *1933 Was a Bad Year*) and appellations (the family name and some character names are different, the town is Roper, not Rocklin). Dom, on his way to California at *1933 Was a Bad Year*'s end, anticipates Arturo Bandini's arrival in Los Angeles at the beginning of *Ask the Dust* (1939).

The most compelling reason why *1933 Was a Bad Year* seems a natural part of the Bandini saga rests in the goal of the protagonist. *Wait Until Spring, Bandini* features an Arturo who dreams of a future bright with baseball glory. *Ask the Dust* depicts an Arturo who dreams of being a great author or, as one critic put it, "of seeing his name on bestseller lists instead of on the roster of a major league team."[18] Dominic Molise in *1933 Was a Bad Year* occupies a transitional state between the dreams of pitching and authorship: though he is desperate for a spot on a major league team, he is more strongly impacted by stories—those he mentally pens for himself and for his family. Reaching between the baseball-dreamer of *Wait Until Spring, Bandini* and the writer-dreamer of *Ask the Dust* is Dominic Molise of *1933 Was a Bad Year:* Dom is an author in the making.

There are a number of places in the novel where Dominic thinks about himself and his life as if it were a story. In the first chapter are two instances of this. When he imagines his future in baseball, he also imagines his death and his contribution to baseball celebrated in print: "the crowds cheering, the pitch sliding across at the knees, the batters coming up and going down, fame and fortune and victory. . . . And one day we shall die and lie side by side in a grave, Dom Molise and his beautiful arm, the sports world shocked. . . . Damon Runyon's four-part biography in the *Saturday Evening Post:* Triumph over Adversity, the Life of Dominic Molise" (*Year,* 13). Later in the first chapter Dominic's father Peter tries to convince him to be serious, not pursue baseball, and instead take up the Molise family trade of bricklaying. Mentally Dom writes a projected life story: "So there it was. The whole book. The Tragic Life of Dominic Molise, *written by his father*" (*Year,* 31; italics added).

A by-product of Dominic imagining his life in terms of a publication is a number of very comic situations. A sardonic tone is readily apparent when he imagines fulfilling his father's desire for a bricklaying son: "The Tragic Life of Dominic Molise, written by his father. Part One: The Thrills of Bricklaying. Part Two: Fun in a Lumber Yard. Part Three: How to Let Your Father Ruin Your Life. Part Four: Here Lies Dominic Molise, Obedient Son" (*Year,* 31). In another, more farcical story, Dominic considers if his father were to catch him at Edna Pruitt's house and imagines his fate in the style of an abridged news item: "Father knifes son . . . Police find murder weapon in snow . . . Distraught father held . . . Blames uncontrollable temper . . . Prominent athlete . . . Heartbroken father tries to hang self in cell" (*Year,* 96). In addition to the humorously absurd aspects of this tendency toward overblown narratives, Dominic does read some stories with stalwart seriousness and respect.

Dominic interprets with the most solemnity those stories that concern his grandparents. Grandma Bettina insults Dominic and America repeatedly in the book. Dom reads her insults in the context of her unhappiness in a foreign place:

> She was lonely, her roots dangling in an alien land. She had not wanted to come to America, but my grandfather had given her no other choice. There had been poverty in Abruzzi too, but it was a sweeter poverty that

everyone shared like bread passed around. Death was shared too, and grief, and good times, and the village of Torricella Peligna was like a single human being. My grandmother was a finger torn from the rest of the body and nothing in the new life could assuage her desolation. She was like all those others who had come from her part of Italy. Some were better off, and some were wealthy, but the joy was gone from their lives, and the new country was a lonely place where "O Sole Mio" and "Come Back to Sorrento" were heartbreak songs. (*Year*, 18)

When Grandma Bettina is heaping insults on him, Dom is not above fighting back and telling her: "Shut up, old woman!" (*Year*, 17). So, though he does not treat her with complete reverence, his spirit is moved by her plight. The pity he has for the memory of his dead grandfather moves Dominic to act reverently, however. Dom is on his way to sell his father's concrete mixer when he has to drive through the cemetery where his Grandfather Giovanni's remains are buried. Seeing his grandfather's grave marker stops Dominic:

> Not that I expected any trouble from my grandfather, for he was dead seven years, but the memory of him was still above the ground. Had he stood there alive, I could have defied him as easily as I had defied his wife in our alley. But he was dead, terribly dead, and I was afraid of his helplessness. I remembered how he used to be when he was on the earth, with fish lures in his crumpled canvas hat, a lover of walnuts and sunflower seeds, how beautifully he sharpened knives, the way he walked railroad tracks from town to town with the heavy whetstone wheel strapped to his back. I remembered how he always sat on his haunches and poked the ground with a stick, not a learned man but a scholar who smiled all the time, pleased to be just a human being in the world. How could I pass? (*Year*, 114–15)

Dominic thinks of the example of his grandfather's life and reads the inscription on the cross—"Giovanni Molise, 1853–1926, Requiescat in Pace" (*Year*, 115)—and cannot ignore its directive to let his grandfather rest in peace. He turns the truck around to return his father's mixer and thereby avoid desecrating the memory of his grandfather by his theft. For Dom there is a certain noble domination that death grants the individual. Though Grandpa Giovanni was himself a gentle man, the story of his simply lived life overpowers Dom; in that moment of remembering, Dom is mentally writing his Grandfather's story. Dom's reverence for stories is reinforced in the cemetery, where lived stories trump baseball dreams.

Ethnicity and Class

As it is in *Wait Until Spring, Bandini,* ethnic difference is a fundamental element of *1933 Was a Bad Year.* It is, however, considered by the protagonist as more of a trade-off than a straight disadvantage. Dominic is poor and ethnically marginalized, whereas Kenny is wealthy and ethnically mainstreamed. Those two traits, ethnicity and wealth, are collapsed in this novel (and in most of Fante's work): consequently, Italian America *is* poverty and Anglo America *is* wealth.

Dominic envies the Parrishes' wealth, while he is also skeptical of its ramifications. The money that Kenny has access to surely gives him more opportunities; already he had been to (and expelled from) prep schools in the East and since his sister attends college, that is no doubt an option for Kenny as well. His expensive clothes buffer the winter, while Dom, who does not own an overcoat, suffers the chill like the landscape around him. One snowy evening under a streetlight Dom describes the bundled-up Kenny: "He stood pink-cheeked under the lamp post, warm as a beaver inside his new coat, his feet in heavy galoshes, confident, free to go anywhere" (*Year,* 92). But, Dom reasons, while Kenny's wealth ensures comfort, it sacrifices toughness. Watching his friend undress in the Elks Club locker room, Dom notices that Kenny has "his sister's features, the same grey eyes and bone structure. I was always surprised at his Dorothy legs, his lean Dorothy waist. His shorts were delicate and frivolous, the things one would expect to find on a girl, and I thought they foredoomed his future as a first baseman" (*Year,* 53).

Since they are so closely identified with wealth, it is significant that, as a family, the Parrishes are divided and distant. In the novel the Parrishes never remain in a room together, but are depicted as always passing each other on their way out the door. Consequently, the Parrishes live among, but not with, each other. Dom observes that Mr. Parrish does not enjoy his wealth. He is "grey and heavy . . . chain-smoking cigarettes, worried about business . . . hating Roosevelt, the Denver papers torn apart and strewn around his chair" (*Year,* 51). The Parrishes live in a "massive brick house . . . a castle," a monument to their wealth; nonetheless, their money has not bought them comfort (*Year,* 46). Dom depicts the Parrishes as appearing under siege. The house is pronounced a "fortress to protect their only daughter." Within the castle daughter Dorothy is indeed protected, but not exactly cherished, and she is assessed as "beautiful as a glacier" (*Year,* 50). The emotional distance of the mother is evident in her inattention to her son. Mrs. Parrish consistently misremembers Dominic's name—out of disregard or straight disdain:

> "Hello, Tony," she'd say.
> "Dominic. Dominic Molise."
> "And what is it Ken says you do so well?"
> "Throw a baseball."
> "I see. Well, to each his own, I suppose."
> And she'd turn to Kenny and say, "Now I don't want you and *Tony* to get into any mischief."
> Out she'd go to her car, driving off to some important meeting. (*Year,* 51; italics added)

To remind the reader of the lifelessness of these wealthy people, Fante gives them a grim name—Parrish, a homonym of "perish."

In contrast to the luxurious coldness of the Parrish household is the rugged warmth of the Molise household, a home life that Kenny covets: "Kenny liked coming to my house. It was old and plain, but he was comfortable there, sitting beside the window in the kitchen, eating a dish of spaghetti or a bowl of minestrone with homemade bread. It pleased my mother to have him asking questions about her cooking" (*Year,* 51–52). Kenny sees a pleasing exoticism in the Molise household:

> He was wild about Grandma Bettina, who buzzed him suspiciously, frowning at his handsome shoes, his tailored slacks and his cashmere sweaters. With folded arms she sat at the table and watched him eat, muttering insults in Italian that Kenny enjoyed but never understood.
> "What's that?" he'd ask. "What's she saying now?"
> And I would translate, "She says you're the son of a whore who's been banged from here to Palermo."
> "Marvelous!" he'd shout. "Beautiful!" And he would leap from his chair and throw his arms around her, trying to kiss her as she slapped him with small hands and ran for her bedroom. (*Year,* 52)

Viewed by the Anglo Kenny, the Molises, particularly Grandma Bettina, are colorful characters. This might come off as patronizing if Dominic himself did not see them the same way. Sharing rooms, trading insults and worry, the Molises brandish their emotions without shame.

Clearly, in *1933 Was a Bad Year* one advantage of being an Italian American is the lively homelife and general emotional warmth. But for Dom, the more prized consolation of this background is the illustrious tradition of Italian American baseball players. During a single attempt to convince his father of the feasibility of his becoming a baseball player, Dom names nine Italian Americans, from Joe DiMaggio to Boots Zarlingo, and points out that they are the "[s]ons of tailors and butchers and fishermen. Of barbers and coal miners. Italian-Americans from homes like ours, from all over the country" (*Year*, 98). The son of a bricklayer would round out nicely this list of pedigrees.

Another advantage that Dominic sees for himself over Kenny is that being not only Italian but poor as well gives him an edge in the long-term baseball dream scenario. As noted, he feels that Kenny's big league prospects are foredoomed by the fact that his underwear is too fine (*Year*, 53). More important, Dominic can name many men who, perhaps because of the obstacles that they had to overcome, made themselves great: "It was always this way with great men, a stirring in their bones, a mysterious energy that set them apart from the rest of mankind . . . They were different. Edison was deaf. Steinmetz was a hunchback. Babe Ruth was an orphan, Ty Cobb a poor Georgia boy . . . Carnegie was a runt like myself. Tony Canzoneri came out of the slums. Poor young men, touched with magic, lucky in America" (*Year*, 53). Here then, is the blessing of the Molises' stultifying poverty, as Dom considers: "[w]ho ever heard of a rich rookie becoming a Ty Cobb or a Babe Ruth?" (*Year*, 12). Dominic reads his family's socioeconomic condition as the stuff that will one day make him great.

1933 Was a Bad Year has not received the same critical or popular acclaim as *Wait Until Spring, Bandini*, though it has not gone unnoticed. Richard Collins has written a very worthwhile essay on the connections between Fante's stories, baseball, and ethics that focuses almost solely on *1933 Was a Bad Year* (Collins 1994). In that essay Collins points out narrative echoes to James Joyce's *Portrait of the Artist as a Young Man* and a thematic angst similar to that in Dostoyevsky's *The Brothers Karamazov.*

For a time a Denver theater company optioned the rights to the novel with the intention of staging it (Spotnitz, 44). Currently, the book is optioned for a motion picture.

1933 Was a Bad Year should be considered among Fante's most accomplished novels, for it not only bears the imprint of Fante's signature talent—sparkling dialogue, humor, and succinct character sketches—it also showcases a mature novelist in full control of his craft.

"The Orgy"

A final version of Colorado boyhood is given in "The Orgy." Like *1933 Was a Bad Year*, the novella was found among Fante's papers and then published with "My Dog Stupid" under the title *West of Rome*. His collected letters do not evidence Fante discussing the work outright and the existence of the story must have come as a surprise to his survivors. In a 1933 letter to his mother, however, Fante does mention memories that parallel the events in "The Orgy" including one trip he took with his father in the mountains outside Boulder where a friend had a gold mine (*Letters*, 42–43). As in "The Orgy," that trip to a mine saw a lot of drinking and some fishing, but no actual mining.

"The Orgy" reworks the anecdote related in the letter home and turns it into a fable of debauchery. Told by a 10-year-old Catholic boy, the action has all the trappings of a mock-epic battle between good and evil. It is 1925, before the Great Depression, and though the child's family is not wealthy, they are comfortable and well fed. His father is the bricklayer Fante describes in other novels but—here is a twist—it is summer and Papa is working; he is in charge of a three-man crew that is building the J. C. Penney store downtown. Papa's friend and fellow bricklayer, Frank Gagliano, is an atheist. As a consequence, Mama detests him. One day when Frank comes home with Papa, Mama bars his entrance to the house with a broom, "like a spear-bearing angel guarding the tomb of Our Lord" ("Orgy," 147). The family dog also hates Frank Gagliano, greeting the man with bared teeth and a deep growl. After Frank leaves the front walk, Mama sprinkles holy water where he stood to cleanse the area of the atheist's contaminating presence.

One of Fante's most curious characters appears in this story: Farley Vincent (Pat) Blivins, called Speed by his fellow workers, a black hod carrier who has worked with Papa for 10 years ("Orgy," 159). An impeccable dresser (he comes to work in a suit and tie before changing into his work clothes) and model employee, Speed arrives at work before the bricklayers to prepare the mortar that they will use for the day. The son, working as a waterboy at the site, describes Speed's mornings: "By eight o'clock he had snaked up and down the ladder to the scaffolding a dozen times, artfully balancing hodfuls of mortar and brick to the masons' work area" ("Orgy," 157). Financially savvy and hopeful, Speed speculates in penny mining stocks and considers temporary his days as a hod carrier: "No money in packing a hod . . . It's just a way of killin' time till I hit pay dirt" ("Orgy," 157). Speed, indeed, hits paydirt, and when his "Shasta Glory" stock goes up, he sells his stock and quits carrying hod. As a gift, Speed gives Papa the deed to a gold mine. Papa is reluctant to accept any gift from the hod carrier he is loath to lose.

"I got something for you," Speed said to Papa.
"You don't owe me nothing."
Speed laughed. "Maybe that's what I got for you." ("Orgy," 163)

When Papa sees his name on the transfer of ownership title, however, his reluctance is forgotten, and he thanks Speed for the gift. Speed advises Papa on how to find gold: dig and pray.

Though he knows it will cause strife at home, Papa has to invite Frank Gagliano to be his partner. Frank, after all, has a truck to take them to the mine, and he even has mining experience. As a partner, Frank's first act is to change the mine's name from "Yellow Belly" to "Red Devil." The mine's name and the company Papa is keeping do not promise wholesome activities. Sure enough, weeks go by and all Papa brings home from his mountain junkets are filthy clothes and brutal hangovers. Mama, furious that Papa, a "good Christian," is spending his weekends with an "evil atheist," also suspects immoral activity, possibly involving women. The son remarks: "Shaking out the soiled blankets Papa brought back, she sniffed them with loathing, holding them at arm's length like dead cats as she dropped them into the washing machine. They were filthy things, wine-stained, damp and disgusting" ("Orgy," 174). Finally fed up, Mama enlists the son as her envoy. To the men's great dismay, the boy is sent to join them on a weekend at the mine.

The mine itself turns out to be nothing but a watery 15-foot hole in the mountainside: "Rusted picks and shovels lay on the muddy floor, long disused and so rotten the handle of a shovel collapsed like a mushroom when . . . stepped on. . . ." ("Orgy," 179). Papa and Frank, it is clear, have not been doing any mining. Nor have they been doing any housecleaning; the cabin is a stinking mess. This disorder is unusual for Papa, who, the son explains, was a poor man, "and that for sure, but I only knew him as a *clean* poor man . . . Yet there he was, on his knees amidst all that squalor, as cheerful as a rat in a sewer" ("Orgy," 178). Proof of carnal immorality soon arrives in the form of Rhoda, a rundown woman in a beat-up Cadillac. When the son returns from a walk, Papa and the woman are gone. The boy wants to know where the woman and his father have gone, but when he asks Frank, the man puts the boy on the wrong trail. Eventually the boy finds Rhoda sitting on a rock at the mine entrance, and he thinks his father must be with her: "suddenly I knew that my father was somewhere close by. I could almost smell him behind one of the trees, or the cluster of boulders beyond the mine, or concealed in the thick manzanita" ("Orgy," 182). All day the men and woman take turns hiding, while the confused boy seeks them. Finally, in the late afternoon, the boy returns to the cabin where Papa sits, drinking wine, and boldly lies that he has been there the whole day. Exhausted by all his searching and worrying, the boy falls asleep on a couch. He awakens at midnight to a dead fire and a dark, quiet, empty cabin.

Outside the atmosphere is the opposite: bright with moonlight and fire, populated, noisy with Frank Gagliano's "drunken gravel laughter," the voice of the woman, and the "roar" of Papa ("Orgy," 187). The boy ventures up the trail toward the mine, "enchanted by the sense of evil" ("Orgy," 186). In the shallow mine shaft, the boy observes Papa, Frank, and Rhoda in the midst of the titular orgy: "cleaving together, grunting and sucking and squirming in the naked heavy slithering of arms and legs, caught up like a ball of squirming white snakes, bodywhite under the moon, grinding on a blanket all knotted together with them, clawing, gasping, groaning" ("Orgy," 186). The boy interprets the orgy as diabolically inhuman: arms and legs slither, bodies knot together, the participants grunt and squirm like beasts. While on one level the boy is aware that he has not stumbled onto actual evil, he nevertheless administers an exorcism. Like the envoy of his religious mother that he is, he returns to the orgy bearing the bottle of holy water that his mother had packed among the sandwiches (she labeled it: "Holy water. Use as needed."). Though the boy feels like a fool, he runs up the trail and into the mine shaft—giving fair warning of what he intends to do, shouting: "Holy water on its way!" ("Orgy," 187). The three adults are surprised and transfixed by the boy's appearance and are "there on the ground still, white and naked and paralyzed, rigid like white dead people" ("Orgy," 187). The boy continues his invocations—"Look out for the holy water! Here comes the man with the holy water! It's powerful stuff!!" The boy douses the adults with the blessed liquid: "I whipped it around, spewing it from the bottle, splashing their dead white bodies. 'It's holy water, folks! It's powerful stuff!' On their faces, their chests, their hairy parts, throw the holy water, drive the devil out, kill the devil, save my father, free my father!" ("Orgy," 187). Now in a frenzy himself, the boy runs away from the scene and into the woods.

Later Papa finds the boy beside a tree and takes him by the hand back to the cabin, assuring him that "Everything's going to be fine" ("Orgy," 187). His father's partner, the boy reasons, is the cause of this: "my father . . . could not have done that, for he was my father and some things were not possible" ("Orgy," 187). Later Frank returns and the

boy exacts his revenge by repeatedly hitting the man with a stick, drawing blood, until Frank says "That's enough" ("Orgy," 188). The story
ends with an understated declarative sentence: "It was daybreak when
we drove home" ("Orgy," 188).

The story fulfills every definition of the word "orgy"; we see in the
story generous amounts of drunken revelry and sexual abandon. The
god in question in the "secret ceremonial rites in honor of a god,"
another aspect of "orgy," is undoubtedly Satan, whose devilish visage is
on the mine's sign, and who takes over the father's face during the orgy
itself. With the climactic scene taking place in the wilderness, one is
reminded of Nathaniel Hawthorne's similarly enigmatic story, "Young
Goodman Brown."

"The Orgy" has so much symbolism that it seems like a fable. Speed's
gift of the gold mine bestows on Papa what seems like false hope and,
ultimately, disappointment. As noted before, initially reluctant to accept
the gift, Papa says: "You don't owe me nothing." Speed's response
seems, in hindsight, cryptic: "Maybe that's what I got for you" ("Orgy,"
163). Speed's final advice to Papa on how to make the mine work is
identical to what Speed just spent 10 years doing in Papa's employ:
"You dig . . . And you keep diggin' . . . Something else you do, is pray.
You pray and you dig, but you dig more'n you pray" ("Orgy," 164). The
narrator describes only amicability between Speed and Papa, but the
outcome of the story—and knowing how hopeless the mine appears—
makes one wonder if telling Papa to "dig and pray" is ironic retribution
for some offstage offense. That Papa and Frank Gagliano neither dig nor
pray can be read as a reason for their failure and, in the eyes of the boy,
their possible damnation. Ultimately, Speed's gift must be read as
morally neutral, though the story's inaudible message seems to whisper
on every page.

Characteristic of Fante's later work, "The Orgy" is tightly arranged
and sparks with energetic characters and dialogue. Author and critic
Bob Shacochis called it an "outright classic" and the story that "converted [him] forever into the Fante fold" (Shacochis, 203).

Chapter Three

A Lover's Quarrel with Los Angeles: *The Road to Los Angeles; Ask the Dust; Dreams from Bunker Hill*

The Road to Los Angeles,[1] *Ask the Dust*,[2] and *Dreams from Bunker Hill*[3] form a loose trilogy. The novels share a Los Angeles area setting, a hero named Arturo Bandini who wants to be a great writer, and a roughly graduated chronology for the protagonist (teens, early twenties, mid-twenties). *The Road to Los Angeles* presents Arturo Bandini in his most outrageous incarnation, or, as Bob Shacochis describes him, "a teenage firecracker of narcissism and appetite" (Shacochis, 202), and he is outspoken about the burdens of living with, and supporting, his mother and sister. Arturo reads, but does not understand, German philosophers, and fantasizes about, but never meets any, women. *Ask the Dust* is Fante's second published novel, the first one set in the Los Angeles that by then had been Fante's home for almost 10 years. Considered by many to be his finest work and most important contribution to American letters, *Ask the Dust* posits an Arturo Bandini who has come from Colorado to live the California Dream and write the great American novel. He chronicles the other hungry new arrivals to Los Angeles while he himself negotiates the realities that are quickly replacing the dreams he had entertained of Southern California living. In *Dreams from Bunker Hill* Arturo Bandini is, finally, well fed. That novel describes the absurdities of writing for motion pictures and the experience of endeavoring to be a great writer and finding oneself a hack. Written in the final years of his life, *Dreams from Bunker Hill* reads like a photo album of both painful and hilarious Hollywood memories.

Fante's trademark vivid settings are very much in evidence in these three novels. Fante, who lived all over Southern California, pays acute attention to the nuances of its heterogeneous communities. Critic Will Balliett argues that Fante, in the Bandini novels, gives "the reader Los Angeles that no other writer, from Chandler to West, ever quite managed . . . he was an outsider who, like most newcomers to L.A., arrived with dreams and ambitions and romance."[4] The Bandini books are distinctive in part because the action takes place in such varied Los Angeles communities: the low-rent harbor, the dilapidated streets and hotels of downtown's Tenderloin and Bunker Hill, the middle-class vacation retreat of Long Beach, Central Avenue's jazz clubs, illusive Hollywood, swanky Brentwood. Into this urban soup, Arturo throws himself headlong. Los Angeles nurtures and consumes Arturo Bandini, tantalizes and rejects him, inspires his disgust and rapture. The city always intrigues him. Place supplies constant energy in *The Road to Los Angeles*, *Ask the Dust*, and *Dreams from Bunker Hill*. In the final analysis, it is arguable whether Arturo Bandini or the city itself is the central feature in these novels.

The Road to Los Angeles

Never able to find a publisher willing to produce the novel after he wrote it in the mid-1930s, Fante was compelled to set aside *The Road to Los Angeles* and get on with his writing life.[5] Fifty years later, when Joyce Fante found the manuscript among her husband's papers, Fante's publisher Black Sparrow Press lost no time in printing the book.

Not a novel for the squeamish, *The Road to Los Angeles* is narrated by an Arturo Bandini whose emotions buzz like open nerves on every page. Arturo is so psychologically anguished that the novel sometimes feels headed for straight interiority. But the harbor area—its landscape, its industries, its residents—so predominates and antagonizes Arturo that he is prevented from living completely within himself. Running full bore, fists up, at the windmills he sees around him, Arturo Bandini takes on his world, again and again, in this darkly humorous novel.

The Road to Los Angeles was Fante's second attempt to fulfill his contract with Alfred Knopf after the publisher rejected *Pater Doloroso*. Working for Hollywood studios at the time, Fante already felt that that occupation was deleterious to his other writing, making his fiction "stale" (*Letters*, 95). In search of a solitude that would ensure finishing his novel, he chose to move to Terminal Island,[6] a fishing town in the Los Angeles harbor. In a 1935 letter to his mother Fante expressed that he enjoyed the "working-man's town" and was pleased to think that social distractions will not be a problem there: "the smell alone will keep my friends at a distance" (*Letters*, 98). To choose such a place over the Los Angeles and Hollywood he had been living in suggests that Fante desired a return to the working classes among whom he felt at home.

Clearly he felt fed up with the disappointments of Hollywood's movies and New York's literary establishment: a desire to rebel against both is evident in his letters, where Fante communicates a nearly gleeful inability to discipline the brashness of *The Road to Los Angeles*'s tone. He tells Carey McWilliams how the book will "singe the hair off a wolf's rear" (*Letters*, 118) and his brother that the book "doesn't mince words" (*Letters*, 129). In letters he boasts that if the book is "too strong; i.e., lacking in 'good taste' . . . it doesn't bother" him (*Letters*, 129). Later on, however, it did bother Fante and he disparages that the book's "vicious quality exasperates rather than interests the reader" (*Letters*, 129).

The Road to Los Angeles takes place in the communities of the Los Angeles harbor, primarily Wilmington but also San Pedro and Terminal Island, towns that rest on a jagged crescent surrounding the port, interrupted in places by waterways that channel ships in and out of the harbor.[7] Fante faithfully renders the environment of the harbor communities: the foggy climate is saturated with the smell of fish, and the inhabitants are mostly immigrants and desperately poor. Wilmington and the harbor area are distinctive from the more commonly recognized Southern California landscape. The weather, for one thing, is cool and wet: "It was bitterly cold that summer night. The fog had begun to blow in. A wind pushed it this way and that, great streaks of crawling white" (*Road*, 152).

The Bandinis—Arturo, his mother, and his sister Mona—occupy a Wilmington apartment; their "real house" lost upon the patriarch's death (*Road*, 17). His mother's main preoccupation seems to be worrying about her son. Mona is involved with her parish church and her desire to be a nun is Arturo's main expressed objection to her. But Mona does not shrink from Arturo's ridicule and proves herself a formidable adversary. Tensions, not excluding sexual ones, run high between brother and sister.

Though not dwelled upon in the book, the father's death impacts the protagonist considerably: it makes Arturo the sole provider for his mother and sister, a responsibility he shoulders with neither relish nor talent. Arturo takes many jobs to support his family, but he is fired from, or quits, them all. In this regard, Arturo's only talent is for quitting his awful jobs with flair. Particularly gruesome are the conditions at a fish cannery. Arturo considers the work beneath him, and his vanity grasps at a method for reasserting itself; he finds his solution by spitting racial epithets at his coworkers (many of whom are of ethnicities more marginalized than his). Arturo resents the responsibility his father has bequeathed to him and dreams of a life of glamour, leisure, and love. During the novel Arturo accomplishes an approximation of this dream life by writing escapist literature. He also escapes by reading tough-guy philosophers such as Spengler and Nietzsche. Finally, after the myriad conflicts become too much for Arturo, he starts a fight with his sister (which culminates in a bloody lip for her) and leaves home to take his chances in the big city (Los Angeles).

Insults and Fantasies

Throughout *The Road to Los Angeles* Arturo insults or patronizes almost everyone with whom he has contact: his mother, his sister, all of his bosses, his relatives, his coworkers, cafe owners. His insults are rhetorical works of art and make for some of the most comical moments in the novel. Arturo rails with splendid venom at home, particularly against Mona, his younger, but not-at-all cowed, sister. When Mona returns from her work at the church, Arturo greets her: "How's Jehovah tonight? What does He think of quantum theory?" (*Road*, 22). Mona ignores him, and Arturo continues his rant: "I reject the hypothesis of God! Down with the decadence of a fraudulent Christianity! Religion is the opium of the people! All that we are or ever hope to be we owe to the devil and his bootleg apples!" (*Road*, 23). Later in the novel we see that Mona shares Arturo's talent for witty and cutting insults. After reading the novel her brother writes, she assesses: "Plain silly. It doesn't grip me. It gripes me" (*Road*, 139). Arturo is, however, the undisputed master of fantastic scorn: ". . . in the name of your monstrous Yahweh, you sanctimonious, she-nun of a God-worshipping pagan nun of a good-for-nothing scum of the earth, don't insult me!" (*Road*, 75). He calls his uncle an "ignoramus, a Boobus Americanus, a donkey, a clod-hopping poltroon with no more sense than a polecat" (*Road*, 39).

Arturo's colorful and haughty insults create conflicts where none exist or make more complicated simple disagreements. Certainly, this compulsion makes his world seem more consequential than he finds it on first glance.

The battles he initiates also seem to satisfy his narcissism. He escapes his trying circumstances by living in a fantasy world where he is loved, admired, and sometimes feared by others. Arturo retreats to his closet (which he only half-ironically calls his "study") to imagine animated the pin-up girls in *Artists and Models:* "I picked my favorite. She was lying on a white rug, holding a red rose to her cheek. I set the picture between the candles on the floor and got down on my knees" (*Road,* 18). Fante makes the scene humorous by having Arturo's speeches of seduction pronounced in the anachronistic style of the King James Bible: " 'Chloe,' I said, 'I worship you. Thy teeth are like a flock of sheep on Mount Gilead, and thy cheeks are comely. I am thy humble servant, and I bringeth love everlasting' " (*Road,* 18). Arturo's fantasy life impinges on his real life when he follows a woman down a darkened street, thinking that he will charm her with an eloquent pickup line, such as: "And what a beautiful night it is; would you object if I walked with you a bit?" (*Road,* 124). When he overtakes the woman and finds that he is too shy to speak to her, he breaks into a run and pretends to himself that he is out for his evening jog. His jog turns into a sprint and another daydream kicks in: "I was none other than Arturo Bandini, the greatest half-miler in the history of American track and field annals" (*Road,* 125). Running down the dark and foggy street, he imagines that he is racing "the mighty Dutch champion, Sylvester Gooch, speed demon of the land of windmills and wooden shoes . . . Would I win? Thousands of men and women in the stands wondered—especially the women, for I was known jokingly by the sports scribes as a 'woman's runner,' because I was so tremendously popular among the feminine fans" (*Road,* 125). Of course, in his fantasy he bests Sylvester Gooch, though in reality he has raced himself into a strange neighborhood, "the long warehouses threw black shadows into the road. . . . I was at the docks now, with the sea across the street" (*Road,* 125).

Philosophy, the Rabble, Authorship

In what appears to be an affiliated inclination for fantasy, Arturo misapplies the notions of Western metaphysics to his life. He does not comprehend Nietzsche, Schopenhauer, and Spengler but he duly borrows their books from the public library. His none-too-subtle understanding of Nietzsche is revealed in a tribute essay he begins to write: " 'A Moral and Philosophical Dissertation on Man and Woman,' by Arturo Gabriel Bandini. Evil is for the weak man, so why be weak. It is better to be strong than to be weak, for to be weak is to lack strength. Be strong, my brothers, for I say unless ye be strong the forces of evil shall get ye. . . . Be strong, lest ye be weak" (*Road,* 29). Though obviously blind to Nietzsche's finer points, Arturo tirelessly plunges through dull philosophical tomes because "he like[s] one growling word after another marching across pages with somber mysterious rumblings" (*Road,* 47). Endearingly honest about his cognitive shortcomings, Arturo recalls that some of the philosophy books are "very hard to understand, some of them so dull I had to pretend they were fascinating, and others so awful I had to read them aloud like an actor to get through them" (*Road*, 85). Critic Elaine Duffy reads Arturo's studies as a caricature of a self-taught proletarian and Fante as lampooning the more high-minded socially conscious depression-era novels that were their own genre when Fante was writing *The Road to Los Angeles*.[8] Fante is certainly lampooning Arturo's self-righteousness in a scene where Mona complains about the smell of his clothes when he comes home from the fish cannery. Arturo defends his odor (one that makes him ill too) as a badge of honor: "I am a writer-worker. . . . I love this smell. . . . I love its every connotation and ramification. . . . I belong to the people" (*Road*, 74–75). Duffy sees his proletarian bravado as another example of Arturo's excesses: "Bandini's exaggerated patriotism and socialist fervor are comical details, like his habit of speaking from a thesaurus" (Duffy, 42).

Though deviating somewhat from Duffy's straight satire reading, critic Fred Gadarphé also sees Arturo's use of political philosophy in *The Road to Los Angeles* as deliberately clashing with the proletarian novels written during the time period (Gadarphé, 66). Arturo's method of invoking references to "European bourgeois intellectuals" Gadarphé interprets as Arturo's attempt to set himself apart from the masses by identifying with "the literary models of bourgeois culture" (Gadarphé, 67). Gadarphé reads this as the "key conflict in th[e] novel, one that separates Fante from the proletarian writers of this period" (Gadarphé, 67).

It is uncharacteristic when, in Arturo's defense of his odor to Mona, he claims to belong "to the people" since he works so hard to distance himself from the masses. In what Duffy describes as his "habit of speaking from a thesaurus," Arturo attempts to distinguish himself from his fellow residents. At "Jim's Place," a cafe that he frequents, Arturo foists a heady dose of his special bombastic brand of absurd condescension:

"Jim, this pabulum is indeed antediluvian."
Jim asked what I meant. . . .
"The steak," I said. "It's archaic, primeval, paleoanthropic, and antique. In short it is senile and aged."
Jim smiled that he didn't understand and [another diner] stopped chewing, he was so interested.
"What's that?" Jim said.

"The meat, my friend. The meat. This pabulum before me. It's tougher than a bitch wolf."

Jim was upset about the steak and leaned forward on the counter and whispered he would be glad to cook me another.

I said, "Zounds! Let it go, man! It supersedes my most vaunted aspirations." (*Road*, 15)

Upon learning that the fellow diner is a longshoreman, Arturo asserts that his is a "poltroonish profession . . . Infested by donkeys and boobs." And then he adds, for good measure: "We live in a world of polecats and anthropoids" (*Road*, 15).

Though Jim and the longshoreman are probably less well read and do hold Arturo's intellect in a certain degree of awe, they also consider him "mildly insane."[9] Throughout the novel, Arturo is alienated from others. His uncle, for instance, declares Arturo "crazy" and a "maniac" (*Road*, 39). Arturo perceives Jim and the longshoreman to be mightily impressed with him, but that they whisper and smile in his direction indicates their derision.

Ironically, it is a member of what Arturo considers "the rabble" who gives him the idea to be a writer. When Jim—who Arturo would certainly include among the "rabble"—asks him if he has ever attempted to write a book, Arturo seizes immediately onto the idea of becoming an author: "That did it. From then on I wanted to be a writer" (*Road*, 28). The notion that he is now a writer gives Arturo both a new interest in his surroundings and a purpose in life: documenting his milieu. Walking outside the cafe, Arturo sees as picturesque the "little Japanese fishing sloops . . . banana boats and old rope and the brooding mysterious smell of the sea at low tide" (*Road*, 29). Soon, however, his neighborhood seems too banal for his grand imagination.

Arturo does not want to be simply a writer, to quietly scribble and scrawl for the love of the craft; he wants to be the world's most famous and revered author. He imagines his loftily titled book, *Colossus of Destiny* (for which he envisions winning the Nobel Award), resting next to a "few indispensable others" such as "the bible and the dictionary" (*Road*, 93). When he begins his novel, he experiences a bliss he never knew before and days pass with him writing during every spare moment. The book is a romantic adventure story starring one "Arthur Banning"[10] who travels the world searching for his one true love. The story's events are as excessive as its author: Arturo consults a dictionary for a list of countries so his alter ego can enjoy scenes of passion in every nation; he writes one sentence that is 438 words long (*Road*, 138); he gives his story three titles: "Love Everlasting or The Woman A Man Loves or *Omnia Vincit Amor*" (*Road*, 129). After overwrought love scenes in every nation, the hero remains unsated, for he never finds his true love. Alas, at novel's end, Arthur Banning suicides after proclaiming: "Ah, sweet mystery of Death" (*Road*, 139).

Ethnicity and More Insults

Envisioning himself a writer grants Arturo the sensation of choice and agency: he pretends he is not from the harbor, but on a writer's assignment there. For example, Arturo tells his boss at the cannery: "Extremely interesting what you say there. A fascinating sociological aspect of the canning situation. My book will go into that with great detail and footnotes" (*Road*, 57). Though writing makes his world seem abstract—in that his surroundings are book fodder and not reality—this fantasy is constantly overwhelmed by the material reality of the stench of the fish and machinery. He describes his first morning at the cannery as having "no beginning and no end. Between vomitings I stood at the can dump and convulsed. And I told [the other workers] who I was. Arturo Bandini, the writer. Haven't you heard of me? You will! Don't worry. You will! My book on California fisheries. It is going to be the standard work on the subject. I spoke fast, between vomitings" (*Road*, 60). His attempt to elevate himself above his circumstances has two motivations. The pretense of "writer" instead of "cannery worker" protects his vanity. His charade is also motivated by insecurity. In his desire to be admired, he creates a more prestigious profession for himself. It is a complicated process, for though his fakery pushes him above his coworkers, it also alienates him. In the book, he is effectively friendless and this loneliness makes him feel embattled.

And when Arturo Bandini feels embattled, he avenges himself without fail and in characteristically creative ways. He feels keenly even the smallest slight and responds with grandiose, sometimes violent, and often misplaced vengeance. The objects of his wrath are frequently bystanding fish or insects—and plenty of both abound in the harbor town: a fly, a cricket, a mackerel, and, in a particularly gruesome scene, an entire colony of crabs.[11] People do not escape Arturo's asperity either. He more than redresses the wrongs done to him by his sister and the Mexican and Filipino coworkers at the cannery. At lunchtime at the cannery, his coworkers come upon Arturo asleep in the sand; they chant,

"Hey writer! Hey writer!" and turn him over (he has fainted from his nausea) so they can favor him with a mackerel down his pants. When Arturo awakens, he responds to his unpleasant situation by biting the head off the dead fish (*Road*, 62). Arturo moves to the lavatory, trying to recover from his prolonged nausea and also trying to strategize a counter-attack: "There were too many cannery workers for a fight ... It had to be something else, some way of fighting without fists" (*Road*, 63 – 64). When an opportunity presents itself, he chooses to fight without fists by using racial slurs against his coworkers, a powerful weapon that he understands from having suffered from it himself. Arturo reasons that hurling racial epithets "would hurt them every time. I knew because a thing like that had hurt me. In grade school the kids used to hurt me by calling me Wop and Dago. It had hurt every time ... It used to make me feel so pitiful, so unworthy" (*Road*, 64). The intricacies of being from an ethnically marginalized group are candidly represented here, but more subtly worked through in *Ask the Dust*. In *The Road to Los Angeles* Arturo Bandini pulls from his quiver insults of rich variety; however, since he wields no consequential power in his life, all of his taunts are utterly self-defeating and succeed only in alienating him further.

Place

Stephen Cooper reads the representations of place in *The Road to Los Angeles* as mirroring Arturo's personal circumstances, and indeed the city's pockets of despair and excitement do match Arturo's outlook.[12] He depends on his surroundings for work, for a place to read (in parks and lonely docksides), for human interaction (which he usually scorns), for "something great to write about" (*Road*, 29). Often, place disappoints or antagonizes him.

For Arturo, the smells of the harbor are simultaneously sickening and evocative. In *The Road to Los Angeles* the smell of fish trails not only those who work gutting or canning them but adheres itself to the fog, floating, resting everywhere. Arturo describes June as the best month because the mackerel are "running ... and the canneries [are] going full blast, night and day, and all the time at that time of the year there [is] a stink in the air of putrefaction and fish oil" (*Road*, 28). Though up close the smells sicken him (as when he works in the cannery), with a little distance the smells represent the international commerce of the harbor: traveling ships, distant seas and ports of call. Arturo thrills at the intricate sources of these scents: "It wasn't one smell but a lot of them weaving in and out, so every step you took brought a different odor. It made me dreamy and I did a lot of thinking about far-away places, the mystery of what the bottom of the sea contained, and all the books I'd read came alive at once" (*Road,* 28).

The structures, private, public, and commercial, also gauge the condition of life in the harbor communities. The Bandini apartment is cramped and shaky, a "two story pink stucco place with big slabs of stucco wiped from the walls by earthquakes" (*Road,* 16). The stucco absorbs "fog like a blotter" so that in the morning the color of the pink building is turned red; stepping onto the staircase causes squealing "like a nest of mice" (*Road,* 16). Arturo tries to make his own space in the small apartment; when he returns home from the library he retires to his "private study, which was the clothes closet" (*Road,* 18). But even in the closet there is no respite from distraction. His mother, who thinks he is committing sinful acts with girlie magazines in the closet (and she is right) protests by sitting on the other side of the closet door (*Road,* 19).

Life at the Cannery

A variety of ethnicities is represented as populating the harbor in *The Road to Los Angeles:* all are poor or foreign-born, or both. Employed by the harbor companies, the people suffer the attendant vagaries of industries ultimately dependent on the whims of nature (the sea, storms, fish migratory patterns). Arturo, describing his Filipino neighbors, says "the Filipino influx was seasonal. They came south for the fishing season and went back north for the fruit and lettuce season around Salinas" (*Road,* 16).[13] Aside from the Filipino population, the book describes the sizable Mexican and Japanese contingencies in the harbor area.

Arturo works among this diverse Mexican, Japanese, and Filipino population at the Soyo Fish Company. Commensurate with their economic desperation is their exploitation: they are overworked and grossly underpaid.[14] Arturo, after being hired at the cannery (through the recommendation of his uncle), describes the "cannery works" with horrific realism: "The corrugated iron building was like a dark hot dungeon. Water dripped from the girders. Lumps of brown and white steam hung bloated in the air. The green floor was slippery from fish oil. We walked across a long room where Mexican and Japanese women stood before tables gutting mackerel with fish knives. The women were wrapped in heavy oil-skins, their feet cased in rubber boots ankle-deep in fish guts" (*Road,* 58). This painstaking description communicates Arturo's first impression of the cannery's ghastly conditions. The cannery reveals itself as even more appalling after Arturo has become a veteran employee: "The work was hard . . . There was no fresh air, not even enough to fill one nostril. All the windows were nailed down by rusted nails, and the glass was cobwebbed and greasy with age. The sun heated the corrugated iron roof like a torch, forcing the heat downward" (*Road,* 86). By describing the cannery with exacting detail, Fante withholds from his protagonist the interiority Arturo desires. The persona Arturo creates for himself—that of being an observer-writer, not participant—is undermined by his work in the cannery. Then, he becomes a "cannery kid" (*Road,* 84). The omnipresent "smell of fish, a shadow that could not be seen but smelled" (*Road,* 73), marks him: "Everybody knew who I was and what I did when they smelled me coming" (*Road,* 84). In one public place, a movie theater, people move away from him because of the fish smell that no amount of soap can remove.

The physical marks of working in the cannery try Arturo's pride, but the mental impact of a job "done without thinking" frightens him. Arturo works at the labeling machine where the task is aligning the cans so that the machine affixes the labels properly. Looking around, Arturo observes the glazed gazes of his coworkers who have the "whipped sad eyes of old animals from a field" (*Road,* 89). Arturo actually sees more humanity in the labeling machine itself, comparing it to a "child" because of its predilection for breaking down, a capriciousness that freezes production in the whole cannery, inspiring "panic" (*Road,* 87).

The cannery in Wilmington shares the dock space with vacationers bound for Catalina Island, a 23-mile distance from the coast. While working at the cannery, Arturo sees through the steam and past the open door the blue bay of the harbor, and the boats and planes filled with people bound for the island. Sitting outside on his lunch break Arturo watches the wealthy people in their expensive cars whisk past the cannery to the Catalina terminal and feels like a "thief peeking at jewels" (*Road,* 90). These brief, maddening brushes with wealth infuriate Arturo and they give him a material contrast against which he can compare his economic limitations. But no matter how distant his fantasies take him, his mental escapades are thwarted by the distasteful necessities of feeding himself, his mother, and his sister.

A Romantic in a Naturalist's Landscape

Once he has tasted the lyrical potential that authorship gives him, Arturo attempts to cope with his surroundings by opting for a more writerly, romantic outlook. One evening a woman wearing a purple coat walks into Jim's Cafe and Arturo feels so drawn to her that he follows her outside. Her gait is "stubborn, brutish," and she walks in a "zig-zag . . . moving from one side of the wide sidewalk to the other, sometimes at the curbing and sometimes almost bumping the plate glass windows at her left" (*Road*, 120). Though suggesting her apparent inebriation, Arturo manages to ennoble her and rhapsodize:

> And I see you now, you woman of the night—I see you in the sanctity of some dirty harbor bedroom flop-joint, with the mist outside, and you lying with legs loose and cold from the fog's lethal kisses . . . beneath the cold yellow light of a single, spotted bulb . . . your tattered blue shoes tumbled sadly at the bedside, your face lined with the tiring misery of Woolworth defloration and exhausting poverty, your lips slutty, yet soft blue lips of beauty calling me to come come come to that miserable room and feast myself upon the decaying rapture of your form, that I might give you a twisting beauty for misery and a twisting beauty for cheapness, my beauty for yours, the light becoming blackness as we scream, our miserable love and farewell to the tortuous flickering of a grey dawn that refused to really begin and would never really have an ending. (*Road*, 156)

Initially an object of desire, on reflection she materializes as an embodiment of worn-out despair. In drifting, dizzying poetic passages such as these, it is easy to recognize parallels to the similarly lyrical and street rhapsodic Beat writers that Fante predated by 20 years. Ultimately, Arturo cannot reconcile his desire for a more romantic, promising life and the depressing, no-future town he perceives in Wilmington.

Arturo Takes the Road to Los Angeles

As the novel comes to a close, Arturo Bandini becomes an increasingly difficult character with which to sympathize. He is, at least, unpleasant to all acquaintances and is especially hateful to the women he blames for most of his problems. He is furious at his sister and mother, for instance, when they do not offer glowing reviews of the novel Arturo writes. His mother objects to the rampant adultery in the book: "I don't think he ought to sleep with so many women . . . He should find a nice clean little Catholic girl, and settle down and marry her" (*Road*, 146). Arturo can assimilate his mother's discomfort with his randy hero's seductions, but that Mona finds the book "silly" is more than Arturo can bear. He returns to read his book and is appalled to find: "It was quite bad. It was worse than that. It was a lousy book. It was a stinking book. It was the goddamnedest book I ever saw . . . Mona is right. It's silly" (*Road*, 149). Arturo alights on Mona's slight—calling his book silly—as the affront he can avenge. With a fury born of displacement, Arturo storms back to Mona: " 'You nun! So it was silly, was it? So it made you laugh, did it? So it was the worst book you ever read, was it?' I lifted my fist and let fly. It struck her in the mouth" (*Road*, 152). Walking out of the apartment, he thinks: "The feeling was that I would never see them again. And I was glad" (*Road*, 152).

Arturo then steals and pawns his mother's jewelry to pay for a train ticket to Los Angeles. The city, though only 20 miles away, represents an entirely new life for him. For Fante there must have been a rite of passage ring—from family boy to young man of the world—to theft from family because it appears in many of his works.[15] In the melodramatic farewell letter Arturo leaves his mother he maintains his hyperbolic rhetoric, perhaps to convince himself of his lofty endeavors. He writes: ". . . living with you and Mona is deleterious to the high and magnanimous purpose of Art, and I . . . am an artist, a creator beyond question" (*Road*, 163). In spite of his boasting, there is little doubt that Arturo leaves as much out of a sense of failure and frustration as out of any sense of his artistic destiny. Seemingly unable to either conquer or coexist with the working class atmosphere of Wilmington, he abandons it. It is an odd conclusion since taking to the road or moving to the big city, as Arturo does in *The Road to Los Angeles,* has all the trappings of the beginning of a novel, not a conclusion. But it ends at a new beginning; Arturo's final action is walking to the depot to await the midnight train to Los Angeles.

It is a problematic ending because it suspends the reader's ability to resolve conflicts: the protagonist reaches the height of selfish detestability—punching his sister and stealing from his mother—on the last few pages, without an opportunity for redemption. In its sense of absolute finality, it recalls the novel within the novel that Arturo writes. Both Arturo and his alter ego Arthur Banning are young men with extravagant aspirations, who ultimately self-destruct.

That John Fante does not redeem Arturo Bandini effectively doomed the book's publishing prospects during his lifetime, but that he never softened Arturo's character, in all the rewrites Fante completed of *The Road to Los Angeles,* demonstrates how committed he was to his unapologetic hero. It is easy to think that mid-1930s America was simply not ready for the provocative and bellicose *The Road to Los Angeles.* Fante himself judged the book to be "fear[fully] honest" (*Letters*, 130). One publisher, however, thought the manuscript "horrible" (*Letters*, 129). Another surviving reader's report declares the book "belligerent" and "truculent" (*Letters*, 149). Clearly, one person's belligerence and offensive truculence is another's honesty and in getting this book rejected so many times and for similar reasons, Fante must have learned that to find a willing publisher, he would need to temper his candor. In a letter to Carey McWilliams, Fante bitterly pledges to "never again write with such unrestraint—all of which goes to prove that it's a poor policy to be honest and that it is much better to be artistic" (*Letters*, 130).

The Road to Los Angeles is a fascinating novel, for itself and as an artifact of Fante's early work. The novel reveals a writer at a creative crossroads. His published stories up to that time were, in the main, sweet, if forgivingly sardonic, chronicles of Italian American life in a small Colorado town. *The Road to Los Angeles* shares traits with Fante's short stories: humor (Arturo's quasi-intellectualism), adept character sketches (of Arturo and Mona, especially), lyrical descriptions of emotion (the gusts of Arturo's megalomania and self-loathing), and setting (the portraits of longshoremen, canneries, and the transitory life of the harbor). The novel's advantages are derailed somewhat by the ending where the protagonist cuts himself off from his family and rides out of the book on a midnight train. There is a sense that just as Arturo is desperately anxious to be heard and loved in *The Road to Los Angeles,* so too was Fante clamoring in this book: to be heard as an author. Fante went on to publish *Wait Until Spring, Bandini* and *Ask the Dust* in the next few years and in those novels we see Arturo Bandini softened. The hero's frankness remains in these later novels, but is mollified; he becomes a humane persona whose vulnerabilities are more clearly articulated.

A happy by-product of *The Road to Los Angeles*'s rejections in the mid-1930s is what that ultimately meant for Fante's Bandini saga. In *Wait Until Spring, Bandini* Fante returned to his Italian American upbringing in Colorado. More important, he brought back one of his most fascinating characters: Svevo Bandini, father, bricklayer, rogue extraordinaire. That Fante kills off the father in *The Road to Los Angeles* performs an interesting symbolic punishment for the author's father's adultery. It is curious too that Arturo effectively reenacts the father's abandonment of his family by leaving them at the end of the novel.

Of course, if one is in a speculative mindframe, the other side of this query wonders what gutsy prose might we have seen if Fante had seen *The Road to Los Angeles* published in the 1930s? Neil Gordon reads *The*

Road to Los Angeles as something of a literary dare that Knopf and the other rejecting publishers were too cowardly to accept: "Fante would never again attain, and never fully realize, the enormous, subversive, sensual, and utterly original power of his first, unpublished manuscript" (Gordon, 28).

In their bold candor, in *The Road to Los Angeles* both Fante and his alter ego shout out for attention. Readers and critics are still divided on the Arturo Bandini in this novel: is he despicable or is he, simply, mercilessly honest? In the final analysis, Arturo is both and bracingly so: Fante makes no excuses for him.

Ask the Dust

Ask the Dust is an exceptional novel. Like its protagonist, Arturo Bandini, it is brazen and lovelorn and delirious and curt and lyrical. Set in Los Angeles, *Ask the Dust* is a panorama of symbolic imagery and historically authentic detail. Its 1939 publication date inserts it into a year full of literary expressions of Southern California. 1939 also saw published Raymond Chandler's *The Big Sleep,* Aldous Huxley's *After Many a Summer Dies the Swan,* John Steinbeck's *The Grapes of Wrath,* and Nathanael West's *The Day of the Locust.* Like these books, *Ask the Dust* reckons with a California that disappoints newcomers. But as customary as Fante's Los Angeles looks at first glance, it eschews the bleak pandemonium of *The Day of the Locust* or the stylized ennui of *The Big Sleep.* In fact, *Ask the Dust* leaves intact a modified version of the California Dream by featuring a hero who weathers his fallen hopes, makes them into art (a novel), and ultimately chooses to remain in Los Angeles. Fante's novel further distinguishes itself from the customary dystopian Los Angeles novels (which scripted the region as the realm of Midwestern immigrants) with its depiction of an ethnically diverse 1930s Los Angeles. Arturo is a young man passionately in love with the written word, with the city he's chosen to make his stand in, and with a woman who dismisses him. Since its republication in 1980, *Ask the Dust* has been Fante's most popular novel and one that many argue belongs in the canon of American letters. A newspaper account described it as a novel "around which a cult has formed."[16]

Ask the Dust and Fante had to wait decades for these accolades. For a long time, it seemed that *Ask the Dust* would simply disappear.

When *Ask the Dust* was first published, its reviews were, in general, good ones. Critics applauded Fante's stylistic finesse with one critic enthusing that the prose of *Ask the Dust* was a "kind of poetry."[17] The *New Republic* called it "inventive" while the *Nation* marveled that the mixture of laughing and crying in the story managed to escape "utter melodrama."[18] The *Saturday Review* offered a less positive review of the novel, but still found the "California locale . . . very effective."[19] Critic E. B. Garside's review was especially positive. He observed that Fante's book not only breathed in life from "a whirligig American existence," but captured the "wonder of life . . . its glory and cruelty" (Garside, n.p.). Garside also ventured that "[Fante] has written his *Werther*, let us hope fervently he can go on to another *Faust.*" Fante commented to his cousin that Garside, who compared him to Goethe, "really understood my book" (*Letters*, 157).

The book's positive reviews did not translate into strong sales, however, and the ancillary obstacles that *Ask the Dust* faced are legendary (discussed in chapter 1). Finally, after being out of print for 40 years, *Ask the Dust* was reprinted and Fante found in this later generation an audience receptive to his poetic novel. In the three remaining years he had left after *Ask the Dust*'s republication, Fante realized that he had finally succeeded in the literary world, a world he had always yearned to convert.

One of the novel's strengths is its incorporation of specific geographic detail. Protagonist Arturo Bandini describes the sights of Los Angeles as he roams its streets and neighborhoods. What he accounts for is generally, but not wholly, low-rent L. A.: downtown's Grand Central Market, Chinatown (when it was a red light district), and the Plaza, a legacy of Mexican California (before it was kitschy Olvera Street). When he describes the swanky Biltmore Hotel, he can only imagine the interior and himself there in a daydream, with a woman wearing a silver fox fur and being dazzled by his recitations of Sanskrit (*Dust*, 13). *Ask the Dust* also sketches the beaches of Santa Monica and Laguna Beach as well as the remote Mojave Desert, source of the sand forever blowing over the city in the novel. The grand geographic reach of *Ask the Dust* sprawls just like Los Angeles itself. Of course, much of the novel is set in the Bunker Hill area.

Bunker Hill, when John Fante came to Los Angeles, was a neighborhood of resident hotels and run-down mansions that had been subdivided into flophouses—Los Angeles's wealthy having long before left for the city's more western areas. The neighborhood perched above downtown on a steep hill, made more accessible by short tramways. At one time there were three tramways, but by the thirties that number was reduced to one funicular railway: Angels Flight. After the urban renewal programs of the seventies and eighties, Angels Flight was gone and Bunker Hill was transformed into skyscrapers.[20] The novel's geographical and historical specificity ensured that *Ask the Dust* would not be forgotten by historians and scholars of the era. Indeed, it percolated as an historical artifact of Los Angeles for years, remembered for its depiction of a bygone epoch and appearing in bibliographical studies of Los Angeles penned by scholars of Los Angeles literature: Lawrence Clark Powell,[21] Carey McWilliams,[22] Franklin Walker.[23] Powell writes of *Ask the Dust* that in it "Fante perfectly evokes the ambiance of Los Angeles in the depression, seedy and hopeful, shaken by the earthquake of 1933, inhabited by little people barely existing on narrow economic margins" (Powell, n.p.). It is worthwhile to appreciate *Ask the Dust* as a time capsule of depression-era Los Angeles, as Powell does; to limit the book to that significance, however, misses the tremendous prose assets of Fante's novel.

The story of *Ask the Dust* goes thusly: 20-year-old Arturo Bandini, last seen in *Wait Until Spring, Bandini,* moves from Colorado to Los Angeles to write the great American novel, fall in love, and become rich and famous.

When he disembarks from the bus and steps onto the streets of Los Angeles, he thinks that what he wants can be summarized in a sentence: "To write a love story, to learn about life" (*Dust,* 18). Arturo has money in his pocket and a suitcase filled with copies of the magazine that published his first story (*Dust,* 48). Now five months into his Los Angeles residency, his desire to experience life and write about it is especially desperate because his money is spent, he remains dismayingly chaste, and his writing resume remains a single story whose title was lifted from a nursery rhyme: "The Little Dog Laughed."

Most of the writing Arturo does goes into letters of appeal. To his devoted mother he writes for money, pretending that he is on the verge of making a fortune and needing only a little for the interim. He performs the same charade to the landlady, to whom he owes back rent: "My agent in New York. He says I sold another one . . . So don't worry Mrs. Hargraves, don't you fret, I'll have it in a day or so" (*Dust,* 14). In both cases, Arturo's rationalization applies: "It wasn't really a lie; it was a wish, not a lie, and maybe it wasn't even a wish, maybe it was a fact, and the only way to find out was to watch the mailman" (*Dust,* 14). Arturo is on the lookout for story acceptances, but, in the beginning of the novel, he is unable to write any stories to send out.

When Arturo is not writing to his mother, he is writing to another parent figure, J. C. Hackmuth, editor of the magazine that printed "The Little Dog Laughed." Hackmuth is based in no small measure on H. L. Mencken, editor of the *American Mercury*. Fante addressed lengthy, frenzied missives about writing—looking for encouragement—to Mencken. Mencken always responded to the young Fante with "cool, laconic, commonsensical" rejections and advice (Fine 1993, 157), and in *Ask the Dust* Hackmuth responds to Arturo likewise. Arturo comments on Hackmuth's responses: "Ah me, but his letters were so brief. A forty page letter, and he replied in one small paragraph. But that was fine in its way, because his replies were easier to memorize and know by heart" (*Dust*, 56). Arturo's devotion to Hackmuth is absolute. Indeed, he worships the man's very punctuation: "He had a way, that Hackmuth; he had a style; he had so much to give, even his commas and semi-colons had a way of dancing up and down" (*Dust*, 56). Hackmuth is like a fairy godfather to Arturo, for he is a respected personage who, by his acceptances, essentially admits Arturo to the world of publishing. The miracle of Hackmuth's gifts is evident when, from two long letters of Arturo's, Hackmuth carves out short stories, giving Arturo much needed money and confidence in his work.

Confidence is something else—like love and money and recognition—for which Arturo is desperate. The lover he finds, Camilla Lopez, the beautiful beer hall waitress, mirrors his emotional extremes and wreaks havoc on his confidence. Together they embark on a relationship wherein they take turns in the roles of sadist and masochist. Arturo idolizes the Mexican American Camilla, but is intimidated by her and ultimately their intimate interludes are disastrous for both of them.[24] Camilla loves the very masculine and misogynistic bartender, Sammy. Camilla and Arturo inflict pain in individual ways: she pronounces her doubts on the subject of Arturo's masculinity (she interprets his sexual intimidation as "queer"), and he casts aspersions on Camilla's ethnicity, but it is Arturo's epithets that repel us more today. Though Camilla makes his heart sing, he cannot seem to transcribe those notes into a story. When it is clear that Camilla and he cannot be lovers, Arturo feels lost.

As an answer to Camilla's question of his heterosexuality, Arturo has a brief liaison with an older Jewish woman, Vera Rivken. One night she inexplicably follows Arturo to his room, sits down at his typewriter, and types out the poetry of Edna St. Vincent Millay. Never having seen her before, Arturo is shocked by her presence in his room and also moved by the poetry she writes. Profoundly and hauntingly lonely, Vera is as desperate for Arturo's affection as Arturo is desperate for Camilla. Before Vera leaves him, she writes down her Long Beach address and invites him to visit her. Within a couple days, he takes a train to Long Beach (20 miles from Los Angeles), and there Vera coaxes Arturo through his first sexual experience. Following that interlude, Arturo walks out to the seashore and is thinking about life, musing over his passage through the rite of sex, when the Long Beach earthquake hits.[25] The deeply moral (and self-absorbed) Arturo interprets the temblor as God's punishment for his adultery.[26] He dashes back to Vera's apartment, the scene of his trespass, and sees the building nearly destroyed and symbolically meaningful in its ruin: only one wall stands and hanging from it, "like a man crucified, was the bed" (Dust, 99). Arturo presumes Vera dead. The next day he returns to Los Angeles with a strong fear of earthquakes and tall buildings, but pleased to know that he is sexually capable.

The people with whom Arturo lives at the Alta Loma hotel are Midwestern grotesques. Immigrants one and all, the residents of the hotel grapple with life away from home. Los Angeles here (and in much Los Angeles fiction) is the last imaginable outpost for their dreams, but is never what its arrivals imagined. They cannot seem to acclimate to a place where the sun never stops beating down, and the day-to-day reminders of their busted dreams never stop reappearing. In many ways, the hotel population is a microcosm of Anglo Los Angeles: when Arturo first arrives there the landlady lets him in only after ascertaining that he is neither Jewish nor Mexican, that he is, in fact, ethnically acceptable. It is significant that Arturo responds to that initial exclusion, as Richard Collins observes, by going on to have affairs with women who are Jewish and Mexican American.[27]

Camilla, described as having a "mad laugh" when Arturo first meets her (Dust, 36), becomes increasingly unbalanced as the novel progresses. After their rocky start, Arturo and Camilla spend evenings together, but one of them invariably insults or hurts the other. Eventually, she is a deeply unhappy and furtive drug addict. After Sammy's tuberculosis compels him to move to the dry Mojave Desert, she tries nursing him, but her devotions to Sammy are repaid with blackened eyes. For months Arturo does not see Camilla and the peace that her absence allows enables him to complete his first novel, a story about Vera Rivken.[28]

Arturo tries, and fails, to be Camilla's savior. After a stint in an asylum, Camilla returns to Arturo ill and frail. When he sees her so sickly, he thinks of ways to heal her. Bolstered by the money from his novel, his plans are grand: "Laguna Beach! That was the place for her . . . I could take care of her and get started on another book . . . We didn't have to be married, brother and sister was alright with me" (*Dust*, 156). To complete the filial domestic fantasy he envisions for himself and Camilla, they buy a puppy. Like siblings, they argue over what to name the puff of a white Collie.

> "Willie," I said. "His name's Willie."
> "No," she said. "It's Snow White."
> "That's a girl's name," I said.
> "I don't care."
> I pulled over to the side of the road. "I care," I said. "Either you change his name to something else, or he goes back."
> "Alright," she admitted. "His name's Willie."
> I felt better. (*Dust*, 158)

Willie calms Camilla. After renting a house on the beach, Arturo feels hopeful: he imagines spending the winter sitting in the upstairs loft writing and Camilla getting healthy again. Before he goes back to Los Angeles to retrieve his belongings and check out of his hotel, he disposes of the marijuana he finds in her purse. When he returns later that night, the house on the beach is dark and Camilla and Willie are gone. Without Camilla, the domestic fantasy evaporates, and he cannot bear to stay in the beach house alone. Arturo returns to Los Angeles to find that his room at the Alta Loma hotel has been rented to someone else. He takes another room, but he is uncomfortable there: "I set my typewriter in one place and then another. It didn't seem to fit anywhere" (*Dust*, 160). A week later, Arturo's debut novel is released, but with Camilla gone, his joy at this milestone is negligible: "For a while it was fun. I could walk into department stores and see it among thousands of others, my book, my words, my name, the reason why I was alive. But it was not the kind of fun I got from seeing *The Little Dog Laughed* in Hackmuth's magazine" (*Dust*, 162).

A postcard from Sammy informs Arturo of Camilla's whereabouts: "That Mexican girl, is here, and you know how I feel about having women around. If she's your girl you better come and get her because I won't have her hanging around here" (*Dust*, 162). With a copy of his newly published novel, Arturo drives to the desert. Sammy points out the direction in which Camilla and the puppy wandered away after he kicked her out, two days previously. It is midnight when Arturo arrives, but he, outraged at Sammy's insensitivity and despairing of finding Camilla, walks after her. Three hours later, when Arturo abandons his hopeless search, he returns to his car for the novel, which he inscribes "To Camilla, with love, Arturo." He throws the book "far out into the direction she had gone" (*Dust*, 165). The novel's last line: "Then I got into the car, started the engine, and drove back to Los Angeles" (*Dust*, 165).

Arturo Bandini and Los Angeles Mythologies

In *The Road to Los Angeles* the harbor is a place Arturo wants to leave, imagining his dreams would be realized elsewhere, in Los Angeles. In *Ask the Dust* Arturo *is* elsewhere, having arrived at a place of his own choosing; this makes the city's rejections all the more difficult. The Los Angeles Arturo perceives and writes about is equal parts the reality he experiences and the dreamy notions he brought with him from Colorado. Against the backdrop of Los Angeles, Arturo wrestles with not only his own dreams, but those of the region at large.

Critic Gerald Managan reads Los Angeles as custom made for the passionate Arturo: "Sprawled between the ocean and the desert, Los Angeles makes the perfect setting for the extremes of his own nature; and it is painted in detail" (Managan, 303). The passions of Arturo first seen in *Wait Until Spring, Bandini* go into high gear in a city profoundly mythologized by civic boosters.

The Los Angeles myth that used to beckon (mostly Midwestern) would-be residents was comprised of a healthy climate, less saturated economic markets (opportunity for more), freedom from the repressive mores of one's hometown, and the paradisiacal landscape of transplanted Mediterranean foliage and sandy beaches. In fiction, Los Angeles is often represented as the American Dream's last gasp—equal components of the dream are optimism and simultaneous fear that the dream is an illusion. As noted previously, *Ask the Dust* was published during an era when disappointment in California prevailed in such novels as *The Day of the Locust* and *The Grapes of Wrath*. A 1939 review of *Ask the Dust* commented on this zeitgeist: "As the background for a special kind of fiction of frustration and horror, Southern California seems to be losing nothing of its fascination . . . contemporary writers are doing little to gild the famous sunshine or paint the odorous orange blossom of the state. . . . This particular vision of a modern inferno continues in the story of Arturo Bandini."[29] Elaine Duffy compared *Ask the Dust*'s depiction of the city to that in Norwegian author Knut Hamsun's *Hunger:* "as

in that great novel, the city in which the hero goes hungry has a singular
. . . presence" (Duffy, 43). While these critics acknowledge the very real,
very threatening aspects of Los Angeles in the novel, what must be
taken into account is how Arturo's optimism thwarts the city's rejections time and again. Ironically, what frequently buoys him is his belief
in the very mythologies that he knows spurious.

Novels set in Los Angeles often portray the city as an absurd place.
Much of the tragicomic energy of both Aldous Huxley's *After Many a
Summer Dies the Swan* and West's *The Day of the Locust,* for instance, is
provided by the absurd behaviors of the people and the bizarre architectural styles of Los Angeles. *Ask the Dust* also foregrounds that tradition
of absurdity in the residence hotel that Arturo moves into upon arriving
in Los Angeles. The Alta Loma Hotel is "built on a hillside in reverse . . .
if you had room 862, you got in the elevator and went down eight
floors, and if you wanted to go down in the truck room, you didn't go
down but up to the attic" (*Dust,* 15). A resident of the hotel exhibits his
own eccentric behavior: "every afternoon when the sun hits the west
side of the hotel, he slept with his head out the window, his body and
legs inside" (*Dust,* 28). Arturo must renounce what he knows is true and
accept his landlady's illogic to gain entrance to his Los Angeles domicile.
When Arturo initially arrives at the hotel his landlady maintains that he
cannot be from Boulder, Colorado, since, she insists, Boulder is a city in
Nebraska (*Dust,* 49). In fact, she will not let him register until he acquiesces that Boulder is in Nebraska, not Colorado.

The novel's ambiance sometimes echoes that of hard-boiled Los
Angeles: a glamorous and enticing, though morally corrupt city. This
Los Angeles is one conventionalized by Chandler, among others, as
bleak and sinister. *Ask the Dust*'s hard-boiled atmospherics are evident
when Arturo "prowl[s] the city" and finds "mysterious alleys, lonely
trees, rotting old houses out of a vanished past" (*Dust,* 152). Nihilistic
Los Angeles is underscored when Arturo reports a morning on a downtown street where "the wet air [is] already bluish from monoxide gas"
(*Dust,* 38). The genre of hard-boiled literature is implicitly emphasized
when Arturo describes walking past Bunker Hill's "horrible frame
houses *reeking with murder stories*" (*Dust,* 12; italics added). But like the
absurd moments of the novel, the hard-boiled elements never take full
control of the atmosphere. Fante complicates and enriches the hard-
boiled stylistics of Los Angeles fiction by positing an engaged, candid,
passionate, and often hopeful protagonist in the midst of hard-boiled literature's conventionally brutal city.

Amidst the city's sinister elements, Arturo holds onto his idealistic visions; when life is going well for him, he reads the city as a straightforward confirmation of his dreams. During a spell of satisfying and productive writing, the rest of his fears subside: ". . . the pages piling up and all other desires asleep . . . wonderful waves of tenderness flooded me when I talked to people and mingled with them in the streets" (*Dust,* 113). Later, after the interlude with Vera where his heterosexual virility is confirmed, he rhapsodizes the city: "I sat in a dream of delight, an orgy of comfortable confidence . . . Ah, Los Angeles! Dust and fog of your lonely streets, I am no longer lonely" (*Dust,* 125). Another time when Arturo is feeling self-assured, he speaks of an "incomparable" evening where "the blue and white of stars and sky were like desert colors, a gentleness so stirring I had to pause and wonder that it could be so lovely" (*Dust,* 119).

Ethnic Mythologies

Upon moving to Los Angeles, Arturo discovers that the social perception of his ethnicity has shifted. While in Colorado his Italian background is not at all considered white, in Los Angeles he is thought almost, but not totally, Anglo. Symbolically, he is between ethnicities: he bridges Camilla's vibrant, romantic, frenzied Los Angeles and landlady Mrs. Hargraves's dissipating, doomed, unhappy Los Angeles. Arturo's is a wildcard ethnicity; that is, he can play his ethnicity in more than one way. At the Alta Loma hotel, he is a member of the community of Midwestern immigrants. In the tortured relationship he shares with Camilla, he sometimes asserts dominance by stressing his slight ethnic advantage over her more castigated ethnicity.[30] When he condescendingly ascribes to her a diminutive mythology (calling her a "Little Mexican princess") she refutes the assignation: "I'm *not* a Mexican! I'm an American" (*Dust,* 61). In spite of her resistance to his reductive categorizing of her, Arturo continues to use racist epithets to temporarily bolster his confidence. He later ups the ante by calling Camilla a "filthy little Greaser" (*Dust,* 44). Outraged, she runs away from him, and then he picks out of the street a "long cigaret butt" and "lit it as I stood with one foot in the gutter, puffed it and exhaled toward the stars. I was an American and goddamn proud of it. . . . From sand and cactus we Americans had carved an empire. Camilla's people had had their chance. They had failed" (*Dust,* 44). Fante parodies Arturo's manifest destiny narrative by placing Arturo in the gutter as he delivers it. A subsequent tirade demonstrates Arturo's firm distrust of the city's powers (which his American pride would initially appear to align him with). Though here he expresses it only to himself, he too suffered from ethnic prejudice when growing up in Colorado: "Ah, Camilla! When I was a kid back home in Colorado it was Smith and Parker and Jones who hurt me with their hideous names, called me Wop and Dago and Greaser, and their children hurt me, just as I hurt you tonight" (*Dust,* 46). Fred Gadarphé notes that the process of ethnic identification that Arturo undergoes in the novel provides an insight into how some immigrants "fashion an American identity through the process of denying other immigrants and their children the same possibilities."[31] In this case, Arturo claims for himself the label "American" while denying that Camilla is an "American." But Arturo's contrition over this put-down and his empathy with Camilla's situation (based on his own experience as an ethnic minority) means that ultimately, he can only align himself against Anglo Los Angeles.

Arturo calling Camilla a "greaser" shocks some readers today. It is therefore instructive to note that Fante had considered drawing Arturo Bandini in a much more sympathetic, what we would call today politically correct, light. A lengthy, never-sent letter that Fante wrote to his editor in 1938[32] shows the many changes Fante eventually made to the novel, particularly to the characterizations of Arturo and Camilla. The complicated relationship between the two is more overtly described in the letter—published as *Prologue to Ask the Dust* in 1990—with Fante making it clear that Camilla is interested in Arturo only as a means to forget Sammy. At one point in the *Prologue* Camilla herself articulates her disgust for Arturo and strange attraction for Sammy: "Sammy was a man, not a silly writer, not a sissy, and I loved that Sammy, and he hated me, oh God he hated me. Because I was a Mexican, he called me Spick, he called me Greaser, he hurt me so. But him! This Arturo, he told me to be proud I was a Mexican." In his letter Fante explained: "Bandini is sympathetic with the girl because he understands this business of social prejudice . . . [Camilla was a] beautiful Mexican girl who *belonged* to the land . . . but was not welcome." On the basis of the *Prologue* we see that for his final draft Fante chose a riskier characterization for his hero—one where Arturo, who himself knows well the pain caused by prejudice, foists it on Camilla when he wants to undermine the sexual power she has over him. The *Prologue* demonstrates what the novel already infers: that Fante was very deliberate in showing both the moral bankruptcy and seductive power of ethnic prejudice.

What Arturo discovers in Los Angeles is that the Anglo-privileging social hierarchies of the Midwest were simply grafted onto Southern California. He sees around him "the same set, hard mouths, faces from my hometown" (*Dust,* 46). Arturo's ethnic precariousness is evident in a scene, noted earlier, when his landlady, who serves as a kind of civic gatekeeper, interrogates him about his ethnicity: "Young man, are you a Mexican? . . . We don't allow Mexicans in this hotel . . . or Jews" (*Dust,* 49). His acceptance in the hotel (hesitatingly granted though it may be) underscores the dubiousness of his ethnicity in Los Angeles overall. This ethnic exclusion emphasizes the existence of the social struggles he mistakenly thought he had left behind when he came to Southern California.

Like city boosters, Arturo is not orthodox about discriminating between Los Angeles's discordant ethnic mythology of Anglos in a Mediterranean paradise. For example, when Arturo sees his first palm tree in California, he thinks of "Palm Sunday and Egypt and Cleopatra," fusing holy land symbols and vaguely pagan exoticism (*Dust,* 16). Elsewhere, with Vera Rivken, Arturo uses the malleable mythologies in a sexual fantasy to embolden his faltering confidence; in the strange playacting that precedes their sexual union, Arturo tells Vera: "I'm a conqueror. I'm like Cortez, only I'm an Italian" (*Dust,* 94). There Arturo wants to imagine himself a conqueror, but to do so he feels compelled to reinscribe history—making himself Cortez, but Italian—so that he can identify with the conqueror. The awkwardness of his pronouncement associatively remarks on the very process of elastic mythologies. Another instance where Arturo collapses ethnicities to fit a mythology is in his perceiving Camilla Lopez a "Mayan princess" (*Dust,* 94). We never learn exactly Camilla's ethnicity, but chances seem good that she is not Mayan. In another kind of mythologizing—this one more romantic— Arturo also parallels Camilla's appearance with the indigenous physical landscape: "she was all of those calm nights and tall eucalyptus trees, the desert stars, that land and sky, that fog outside" (*Dust,* 123). To Arturo, Camilla embodies his antithesis: whereas he is a recent arrival, she is "deeper rooted"; where he came to Los Angeles with "no purpose save to be a mere writer," Camilla, by virtue of her romanticized ethnicity, belongs there. Arturo equates her Mexican background (in this formerly Mexican province) with regional authenticity.

Ask the Dust's Midwesterners and More Myths

Ask the Dust accounts for the experience of the Midwestern immigrant's disillusionment that is so prevalent in Los Angeles literature, and since the speaking narrator is himself an immigrant, the immigrant experience sways the outlook of *Ask the Dust.* Arturo describes the conditions of the Midwestern migrants he sees around him: "they sold their homes and their stores, and they came here by train and by automobile to the land of sunshine, to die in the sun, with just enough money to live until the sun killed them . . . tore themselves out by the roots in their last days, deserted the smug prosperity of Kansas City and Chicago and Peoria to find a *place in the sun*" (*Dust,* 45; italics added).

The migration itself here resembles a mythic morality play. The areas left behind, "Kansas City and Chicago and Peoria," localize the trope "smug prosperity." And Southern California represents the site of an American tragedy: a "place in the sun." The immigrants themselves are guilty of pursuing impossibility and venturing to a place that is too fantastic to be real, that will only disappoint their dying days. This passage parallels the criticism later offered in a book by Fante's good friend Carey McWilliams. McWilliams describes this longing for the home left behind as a "typical American" experience: a "nostalgia for an America that no longer exists . . . that former Kansans, Missourians, and Iowans literally gaze back upon, looking backward over their shoulders" (McWilliams, 179). McWilliams's and Arturo's takes on the Midwestern migration overlap. Arturo reads the Midwestern migration to the West Coast as a ludicrous scramble for a dream that results in an inevitable and uneasy synthesis: a zealous devotion to Southern California and a fierce yearning for home.

Arturo portrays the "new Californians" as anxious to maintain a belief in the fantasy that initially drew them to Southern California. These immigrants have "a few dollars in the bank . . . enough to keep alive the illusion that this was paradise, that their little papier-mâché homes were castles" (*Dust,* 45). He goes on to describe people who, bewitched by motion picture glamour, no longer see their actuality but "stagger out of movie palaces and blink their empty eyes in the face of reality" (*Dust,* 47). These "empty-eyed" individuals are similar to those who populate West's *The Day of the Locust.* Perhaps they are less grotesque and granted a more empathetic portrayal in *Ask the Dust* since Arturo often identifies with them. In a sarcastic address to his fellow bachelor migrants, Arturo declares: "After a while, after big doses of the *Times* and the *Examiner,* you too will whoop it up for the sunny south. You'll eat hamburgers year after year and live in dusty, vermin-infested apartments and hotels, but every morning you'll see the mighty sun, the eternal blue of the sky . . . and the hot semi-tropical nights will reek of romance you'll never have, but you'll still be in paradise boys, in the land of sunshine" (*Dust*, 46). In short, the converted illustrate a paradox: though their everyday lives are characterized by poverty and desperation, their own dreams and the sunny climate conspire to convince them of the viability of Southern California's mythology.

Arturo ruminates on the sway Southern California mythologies have over the national imagination. His own migration from Colorado to Los Angeles corroborates the fascination the United States has for California. So it is personal experience that fuels his distaste for the media culture that propagates images of a fantasy California: "You can't fool the folks back home . . . they know what California's like. After all, they read the papers, they look at the picture magazines glutting the newsstands of every corner in America" (*Dust*, 46). At this point in the narrative, a disillusioned Arturo counts himself as a "new Californian," one who is distinct from "the folks back home." The mythology of Los Angeles—a place for opportunity for all, which the existence of the poor denies—is a version of the American Dream mapped onto the West Coast. Arturo comments on this connection to the American Dream when he reworks the term "plenty" (as in, land of) by describing his only bounty as "plenty of worries" (*Dust*, 27).

Ask the Dust's Dust

The metaphysical axis of this novel is in its title: *Ask the Dust*. The trope of dust powders this text: this book is lousy with dust. Fante uses the word repeatedly, in a staggering variety of ways, but the overall significance points to both mortality and the human experience itself. Dust is also the literal sign of the land, which the immigrants to California can never fully shake. Arturo describes people as having the "dust of Chicago and Cincinnati and Cleveland on their shoes" (*Dust*, 45). Because the pre-California homeland is often imbued with the glow of innocence, a place people were foolish to abandon, the roots that the migrants severed symbolize their fall. Dust is the permanent residue of this mistaken uprooting.

In the novel, dust is often associated with the Anglo culture of Los Angeles. The exclusionary practices of the Anglos are embodied by Mrs. Hargraves, who initially denies Arturo entry into her hotel. Mrs. Hargraves's alignment with dust is evident in her dusty tea and her cookies, which according to Arturo, tasted like "death." Also, her apartment is described as a "well-dusted tomb" implying not only that she lives in her own coffin, but that dust is often cleaned from the room or, if "well" means "much," even that dust covers the room. Though from Connecticut, she is grouped together with the midwestern Anglos, "The old folk from Indiana and Iowa and Illinois" (*Dust*, 45), who came to California to die. Granules of sand from the desert comprise another, more aggressive dust that symbolizes Los Angeles's doom: "The desert was always there, a patient white animal, waiting for men to die, for civilizations to flicker and pass into darkness" (*Dust*, 120). Dust features prominently in the descriptions of the Long Beach earthquake and the earthquake's aftermath. Arturo watches and feels the ground move and realizes, "It was an earthquake. Now there were screams. Then dust. Then crumbling and roaring. . . . Chimneys toppled, bricks fell and a grey dust settled over all. . . . I said a prayer but it was dust in my mouth" (*Dust*, 98–99). "The whole world was dust and dust it would become" (*Dust*, 104). For Arturo, the dust rising from the temblor's rubble represents a pre- and post-Los Angeles eternity: the city itself a temporary addition to the landscape.

The metaphor of dust in the form of the biblical symbol of physical being ("ashes to ashes, dust to dust") runs through the text. Sammy, the now tubercular bartender who is Camilla's unrequiting lover, ails in self-imposed exile in his Mojave Desert shack. Arturo describes him as "a man like myself, who would probably be *swallowed by the desert* sooner than I" (*Dust*, 120; italics added). The desert later serves as the apparent cemetery for Camilla, who disappears there after Sammy banishes her from his shack. Arturo goes in search of Camilla in the desert. While looking for her Arturo observes: "The sandy earth revealed no footstep, no sign that it had ever been trod. I walked on, struggling through the miserable soil that gave slightly and then covered itself with crumbs of grey sand. You could die, but the desert would hide the secret of your death, it would remain after you, to cover your memory with ageless wind and heat and cold" (*Dust*, 163–64). Arturo interprets the mythic significance of the desert—in conventional high modernist terms—as a "wasteland" (*Dust*, 164). As he searches the desert for Camilla, Arturo perceives in the vast expanses "a desolation . . . a supreme indifference" (*Dust*, 164). The desert too is where the book ends—with Arturo hurling a signed copy of his first published novel into the desert in the direction Camilla had gone. That the story ends in the desert flags again the dust's association with mortality. At the novel's close, the desert's sands will, it can be presumed, cover both Camilla's body and the thrown novel.

Ask the Dust is, by far, Fante's most popular and critically acclaimed novel. Over the years, a number of production companies have

expressed interest in bringing the story of Arturo Bandini and his Los
Angeles to the screen, though none, to date, have followed through. A
Robert Towne screenplay awaits cameras.

Though in poor health in 1980, Fante savored the attentions critics
and readers paid *Ask the Dust.* After the novel's republication, a journalist reported that Fante was "enjoying—to put it mildly—the new success of 'Ask the Dust'" (Warga, 5). Fante said: ". . . what pleases me
most is to be hearing from so many people and to know the damn thing
has stood up to the test of time" (Warga, 5).

It is fitting that *Ask the Dust* would prove to be such an important
novel for Fante's late-life fame, for it was his best and favorite son.

Dreams from Bunker Hill

John Fante's final novel, *Dreams from Bunker Hill,* reproduces the raucous
Hollywood of his early screenwriting days in the 1930s. In an interview
at the end of his life, he talked about this period when he knew William
Faulkner well and met Sinclair Lewis and F. Scott Fitzgerald on the
streets of Hollywood.[33] In *Dreams from Bunker Hill* Fante depicts many of
the writers with whom he worked and, more frequently, cavorted.
Among them were Nathanael West, Dalton Trumbo, and Frank Fenton,
writers brought to California by Hollywood opportunity. The memories
of these talented authors haunt the studio hallways of *Dreams from
Bunker Hill* and appear in restaurants Musso-Frank's and Chasen's, the
Stanley Rose bookshop, in a movie studio cafeteria. The story is a string
of energetic vignettes about a young short story writer who loses himself
in hack Hollywood and then tries to recover the serious writer he once
was by taking to his heels and running.

The lively tone of the episodes is remarkable in light of Fante's poor
health at the time of its composition. For years he had suffered from diabetes and by the late 1970s the disease had taken both his legs and
then, finally, his eyesight. As sick as Fante was, he was jubilant when
Black Sparrow Press republished *Ask the Dust* in 1980, and he thrilled to
"be hearing from so many people" (Warga, 5). Fante's spirit was so
buoyed by the attention that *Ask the Dust* received, his interest revived
in a book he had been dictating to his wife (originally entitled *How to
Write a Screenplay*). And so *Dreams from Bunker Hill* came to be. Because
he was blind, the novel had to be dictated to Joyce. In a 1978 letter to
Carey McWilliams, Fante explained the difficulties of writing blind:

"My sight is gone and I spend considerable time trying to fashion another novel. The transition to blindness is not easy. It is a matter of intense concentration and a dependence on memory" (*Letters*, 308).

In *Dreams from Bunker Hill* Fante returned to Arturo Bandini, and the protagonist is only a few years older than he had been in *Ask the Dust*. Fante had kept Arturo out of Hollywood for years, as if he did not want to taint his beloved alter ego with the Technicolor disappointments of his own years as a screenwriter. Fante's dislike for Hollywood is well documented.[34] In a 1938 letter to his cousin he discussed a draft of *Ask the Dust* and pointedly commented that it is a "Los Angeles" story, "(no Hollywood stuff)" (*Letters*, 151). In spite of Fante's earlier reluctance, bringing Arturo to Hollywood turned out to be a nice piece of poetic justice for Fante. As combative as Arturo is, he gives Hollywood hell.

Although *Dreams from Bunker Hill* does not make reference to events in other Arturo Bandini books, the novel feels as if Fante picked up the drama of Arturo Bandini's life when we had last seen him in *Ask the Dust*. He is still living on Bunker Hill, writing long letters and short stories for his editor-mentor (here called Heinrich Muller; in *Ask the Dust*, J. C. Hackmuth; in Fante's life, H. L. Mencken). Arturo narrates this story of how, again, he struggles to become an author. When the novel opens he is paying bills by logging hours at a downtown cafe: "I was a busboy nonpareil, with great verve and style for the profession" (*Dreams*, 9).[35] Arturo's small triumphs in the short story trade make good copy for a drunken journalist who stumbles into the cafe one day, photographs him serving a young woman, and prints up a brief story for his newspaper. This was an actual event taken out of Fante's life. In August of 1933, Fante's photograph was printed in the Los Angeles *Examiner* along with a headline that read: "Literary Dish Juggler: Bus Boy During the Day, at Night He's Author."[36] The newspaper anecdote is the first of many events from Fante's life—documented elsewhere—that appear in *Dreams from Bunker Hill*.[37]

Arturo's brush with fame leads to a job offer from a literary agent who hires him as an assistant editor. Arturo's job is to salvage what he can from vanity manuscripts written by moneyed authors. His first assignment is a short story, "Passion at Dawn," written by Jennifer Lovelace (*Dreams*, 12). Soon he is "hacking away" at the tale: "the story of six school teachers riding in a covered wagon across the plains, having skirmishes with Indians and outlaws, and finally arriving in Stockton" (*Dreams*, 15). Arturo's acceptance of the position marks the first time he uses his art as a salaried job. Ultimately, it initiates the slippery slide down his writing takes during the course of *Dreams from Bunker Hill.*

In the novel's first five chapters, Arturo traipses through downtown Los Angeles. Though this is the world of bars and prostitution, it is presented as a kind of whimsical, if seedy, playland. This fanciful take on frowzy entertainments is evident when Arturo describes stripper Ginger Britton dancing: "Her long red hair hung to her hips, her Valkyrie breasts flying about in wild circles. The audience cheered and whistled. They angered me. Why were they so fucking vulgar? They were watching a work of art with the same acclaim as a boxing match. It was sacrilegious . . . I couldn't bear it, and stomped out of the theater" (*Dreams,* 31). Another example of the rather comical underbelly of downtown Los Angeles is embodied in the prostitute who lives across the hall from Arturo. When business is slow she reads Emile Zola's *Nana* and munches on apples (*Dreams,* 29).[38] She apathetically offers her services to Arturo: "Would you like to see me?" (*Dreams,* 18). But Arturo, who is intimidated anyway, is chilled by her lack of performed interest and does not take advantage of the proposal.

Soon he finds that a less intimidating romance is possible within the hotel. Mrs. Brownell, the landlady, offers Arturo mince pie soaked in brandy, and this gesture proves to be an easier come-on for Arturo to handle. Arturo and his landlady become lovers. A widow from Wichita, she is five years older than his mother. Arturo assesses: "We were good for each other, Helen Brownell and I. Every night I found the passage to her room an easy journey. . . . We shared the darkness together, sometimes, that is. Sometimes I groped a little and she responded. Mostly she was like a relative in the night, a maiden aunt. . . . In the morning I awoke to the hiss of bacon, and saw her over the stove, cooking my breakfast" (*Dreams,* 33). The motherly aspects of Mrs. Brownell are clear—she comforts and feeds Arturo. That this mother figure is also a romantic and sexual partner begs the Oedipal question.[39]

Mrs. Brownell's comforts do not keep the curious Arturo off the downtown streets. In Pershing Square, Arturo gets drawn into a chess game with a master who plays, and beats, eight men at one time. Arturo describes the chess master, Mose Moss: "one man, an old man, a raucous, insolent brilliant man in shirt sleeves, dancing about as he moved from player to player, making a chess move, delivering an insult, then moving on to the next player" (*Dreams,* 37). Arturo feels he can hold his own as a chess player, but that he might falter in the face of Moss's "scatological attack" (*Dreams,* 38). As it turns out, Arturo is insulted in many ways since while the man is mocking him, Mose Moss is also winning every game: "He began to toy with me. It was cruel. It was brutal. It was sadistic. He offered to engage me without his queen, and I lost. Next he removed his queen, his two bishops, and his two knights, and I lost again. Finally he stripped his forces down to just pawns. By now a crowd three deep was gathered about us, howling with laughter as his pawns mowed my pieces down and he worked another checkmate" (*Dreams*, 38). The police arrive and tote Arturo and Moss off to jail for loitering. Stuck overnight in the drunk tank, they play on Moss's miniature chess set and Moss keeps extending Arturo's credit. By the end of the long night Arturo owes Moss $30,000.

Arturo is penniless but for the few dollars Mrs. Brownell slips into his pockets. During his time with Mrs. Brownell on Bunker Hill, Arturo receives a call from a movie director who wants to employ him as a scriptwriter. The unsolicited phone call, placed on the merits of Arturo's association with Heinrich Muller, serves as his springboard into the posh misery of Hollywood screenwriting.

Arturo's job at the studio is an "unfathomable mystery" (*Dreams*, 45) since he is never actually assigned to write anything. Encounters with respected writers who have moved to Hollywood—Nathanael West, Ben Hecht, Dalton Trumbo, Horace McCoy, Sinclair Lewis—leave Arturo ambivalent and alienated. His one friend, Frank Edgington, is wholly jaded by his experience in Hollywood. Arturo describes him as "an Eastern writer . . . He had contributed to the *New Yorker* and *Scribner's*. He hated Hollywood. He had been in pictures for five years, loathing every minute of it" (*Dreams*, 46). When Arturo asks Frank why his dislike of Hollywood does not compel him to leave, Frank replies without hesitating: "Money. I love money" (*Dreams*, 46). Arturo spends his days sitting in his office, waiting for an assignment. He wants "to be brilliant on paper, to turn fine phrases and dig up emotional gems" (*Dreams*, 48). The frustrations of being hired to write and not being permitted to write are mitigated by the salary ($300 a week; as a busboy he made a dollar a day, plus meals and tips), but even cashing his first paycheck does not eliminate his unease and, in fact, leaves him "with a new sensation, a feeling of bitter joy" (*Dreams*, 49).

Arturo, now a "successful Hollywood writer, without even writing a line" (*Dreams*, 49) spends most of his time with Frank. Arturo describes his friend: "He loved the flip side of Hollywood, the bars, the mean streets angling off Hollywood Boulevard to the south. . . . We drank beer and played pinball games. Edgington was a pinball addict, a tireless devotee" (*Dreams,* 47).[40] At work Frank, an obsessive player of children's games, invites Arturo to play pick-up-sticks, old maid, and Parcheesi (*Dreams,* 46–47). At Frank's house the games continue: Ping-Pong, tiddlywinks, darts, bingo (*Dreams,* 69). Frank represents what Arturo could become: a talented author whose disappointments outnumber his successes and whose decisions are based solely on money. For Frank, who seems bested by the studio system, winning games takes the place of success in his career. The screenwriter's experience within the infamously absurd economy of Hollywood prevails in its standard form here: paid well for doing nothing, screenwriters run the simultaneous risk of finding themselves being paid nothing for jobs well done.

While Arturo is becoming more involved with Hollywood, his relationship with Mrs. Brownell is crumbling. One night when they are out on the town, a waiter mistakes Mrs. Brownell for Arturo's mother. She is mortified and that same night breaks off the affair. Arturo moves from his Bunker Hill apartment to Frank Edgington's house. Hollywood becomes his whole world.

Working as a screenwriter is surreal, and his frustrations with his amorphously delineated position only increase: "As time went by I felt like an orphan, a pariah, non-productive, unknown and exiled" (*Dreams,* 70). When Arturo hears that the studio might bid on Theodore Dreiser's *The Genius* and that he might write the adaptation, he begins work immediately. After weeks of work, the deal falls through. After he realizes that his work was for naught, his frustration erupts, and his tears elicit the sympathy of the previously disinterested secretary. When Arturo is then caught with the secretary on his office floor, he is fired by his boss (who, Arturo learns, is the secretary's husband).

Arturo finds freelance work, but it offers a new set of frustrations for him. He is hired to collaborate with Velda van der Zee on a western, *Sin City.* The story, set on the Wyoming plain, features a sheriff, a malevolent Indian chief, a minister, and his lovely daughter. The material is as pastiche as Arturo's collaborator. Velda is the widow of an oil tycoon and her employ in Hollywood appears to be motivated by a desire to rub shoulders with the movie star crowd. In Velda's first words to Arturo, he is made painfully acquainted with her celebrity fixation: "You look like Spencer Tracy. I saw Spence this morning at Musso-Frank's. We had breakfast together. He was telling me about working with Loretta Young—how he loved it. She's really gorgeous, don't you think? I know Loretta and Sally and their mother. Such a lovely family

. . . We used to lunch together, Loretta and I and Carole Lombard and Joan Crawford. You'd love Joan!" (*Dreams,* 79). Velda takes advantage of every opportunity that arises for name-dropping. Even a matter as mundane as a stain on her car's upholstery is transformed into a story of Velda and her famous friends: "You're looking at that brown spot, aren't you? Claire Dodd did it. I took her home from a party at Jeannette McDonald's and she spilled a glass of wine on it. Poor Claire! So humiliated!" (*Dreams,* 81).

After weathering two days of Velda's star-studded anecdotes, Arturo abandons their collaboration and opts instead to write the first draft solo and then send it to Velda for fine-tuning. When he completes it, he considers his screenplay of *Sin City* the "greatest goddamn western story ever written" (*Dreams,* 88). But after he reads the changes Velda makes, he sees that none of his own writing remains. Frustrated again, Arturo has his name removed from the script. Later, when he sees a screening of *Sin City* at a movie theater, he bitterly observes: "In only two places did I come upon lines that I might possibly have written . . . the first was in an early scene when the sheriff rode into Sin City at full gallop and brought his horse to a halt at the saloon, shouting 'Whoa!' Now I remembered that line: 'Whoa!' My line. A little further on the sheriff stalked out of the saloon, mounted his horse, and shouted 'Giddyup!'. . . Whoa and giddyup—my fulfillment as a screenwriter" (*Dreams,* 127). Arturo is disappointed that his work was again for naught and glad that the audience is not entertained by the film. But beyond his own personal despair he recognizes the disheartening nature of the occupation and feels "sorry . . . for all writers, for the misery of the [screenwriter's] craft" (*Dreams,* 127). The studio apparently thinks *Sin City* satisfactory and Velda is given a movie of her own to direct.

That Velda is rewarded for her mediocrity signals a system awry to Arturo and her promotion indicates that to get ahead in motion pictures, he would have to leave his art behind. Instead, he opts to leave Hollywood behind and pursue his art elsewhere. Arturo packs his belongings, punches Frank in the nose, and moves to Terminal Island.

Terminal Island—a place of "white sand" and "weatherbeaten beach houses" (*Dreams,* 47)—is picturesque. Arturo rents a fisherman's shack and thinks to himself: "This place was paradise. . . . I could hear the sea. It came whispering, saying shshsh. . . . Sometimes I heard the bark of seals. I stood in the door and watched them in the shallow water, three or four big fellows playing in the soft tide, barking as if to laugh" (*Dreams,* 101). The description of Terminal Island here contrasts sharply with its representation in *The Road to Los Angeles* (discussed earlier in this chapter). The canneries exhaust and nauseate Arturo in *The Road to Los Angeles* because he lives amongst them and works in one. By contrast, in *Dreams from Bunker Hill* Arturo sees the canneries from afar. He describes the "cannery settlement" as being a mile away, "teeming with workers, men and women, emptying the fishing boats, dressing and canning the fish in big corrugated buildings. They were mostly Japanese and Mexican folk from San Pedro" (*Dreams*, 102). In contrast to *The Road to Los Angeles*, in *Dreams from Bunker Hill*, the canneries enhance the quaintness of his quiet village retreat.

Initially, the city's diversions seem a world away. It is the off-season for fishing. Arturo has the beach to himself, and he spends his time like a man of leisure. He takes silent walks on the beach with his Japanese landlady (neither of them speaks the other's language). In the afternoons he rows a boat across the channel to the library at San Pedro. He also fishes for "corbina and mackerel and . . . halibut" (*Dreams*, 102). In the evenings, he sits in the warmth of a woodstove fire and reads "Dostoyevsky and Flaubert and Dickens" (*Dreams*, 102). In two months Arturo regains the peace of mind he had lost in Hollywood, but does no writing.

The peace of two months comes to a calamitous end when a professional wrestler—the Duke of Sardinia—moves in next door. The Duke is a walking maelstrom of irascible temper expressed in broken English. Soon Arturo is hacking again, this time writing very bad poetry for the Duke's lady love: "O paramour of New Hebrides/Beseech me not to deride thy trust./Love's a strophe amid the bloom of lost heavens./Bring me the weal and woe of scattered dreams" (*Dreams*, 108). The Duke is delighted with the poem: "She'sa beautiful. I take" (*Dreams*, 108). Later, when the Duke's girlfriend arrives for a visit, Arturo cannot resist making a pass at her. Arturo has to speedily pack his belongings into his car. As he drives away, he can see the Duke is close behind, infuriated and in pursuit.

After leaving Terminal Island, Arturo goes back to Bunker Hill and Mrs. Brownell, his former lover. But Mrs. Brownell is adamant about not reuniting and sends him away. Since he is now cut off from Hollywood, Bunker Hill, and Terminal Island, Arturo feels that the entire region has forsaken him: "What am I doing here, I asked. I hate this place, this friendless city. Why was it always thrusting me away like an unwanted orphan? What did it have against me?" (*Dreams*, 132). Not able to find a place to return to in Los Angeles, Arturo reaches farther back—to the place where he cannot be an orphan—to his hometown of Boulder, Colorado. There, Arturo is welcomed by his family and sits down to a dinner of homemade lasagna. His family is impressed with his expensive clothes and fabricated stories about his movie star friends. His sister Stella asks him:

> "[D]o you know Clark Gable?"
> "Very well—a good friend of mine."
> "Is he really that nice? Is he stuck up?"
> "He's as shy as a bird." (*Dreams*, 136)
>
> Arturo's father wants to know about Tom Mix:
> "You ever see him?"
> "At the studio every day. Him and Tony" (*Dreams*, 137).[41]

Arturo's return to Boulder is not the seamless reuniting that he had imagined it would be. In a rush of nostalgia, he visits the library and peruses the authors that "changed [his] life: Sherwood Anderson, Jack London, Knut Hamsun, Dostoyevsky, D'Annunzio, Pirandello, Flaubert, de Maupassant" (*Dreams*, 139). Arturo then runs across a friend from high school who does an interview with him. Like the newspaper piece in the Los Angeles newspaper, this one includes a photograph, but the tone of the piece is mixed: "It was not a flattering interview, nor was it unkind, but there was a challenging quality to it" (*Dreams*, 139). Arturo also interprets a party invitation from the daughter of a wealthy family as mixed and probably extended to test his success in Hollywood and, perhaps, see him squirm. At the party, Arturo becomes his worst nightmare of Hollywood superficiality; after a series of drinks, he name-drops like Velda van der Veer: "Ginger Rogers is a superior person. She has charm and beauty and talent. I regard her as one of the great artists of our time. However, my favorite star is Norma Shearer . . . I play golf with Bing Crosby and Warner Baxter and Edmund Lowe. I play tennis with . . . William Powell and Pat O'Brien and Paul Muni . . . I swim with Johnny Weissmuller and Esther Williams and Buster Crabbe" (*Dreams*, 142). Finally, after initiating a fistfight with a football player, he leaves the party and stumbles home in the snow, bloody and cold. He determines that the entire Boulder trip is a disaster, so he packs his bags, says a good-bye only to the brother who drives him to the bus station, and abandons his hometown in the middle of the night.

With nearly all of his screenwriting earnings spent and no job prospects, Arturo's return to Los Angeles reprises his first arrival. A three-day bus ride later, Arturo is back in the city he had abandoned with $17 remaining in his pocket. He alights for Bunker Hill, this time imagining that perhaps he and Mrs. Brownell (he never does call her by her first name) should get married and move to the suburbs. When he arrives, however, he is told that Mrs. Brownell had died of a stroke the week before. Distraught, broke, and now truly friendless, Arturo moves to a room in downtown Los Angeles and is faced with the typewriter he has not touched in months. Fearful that any writing talent he once had is gone, he says a prayer to Knut Hamsun ("don't desert me now") and starts to write. What he taps out is Lewis Carroll's "The Walrus and the Carpenter":

> "The time has come," the Walrus said,
> "To talk of many things:
> Of shoes—and ships—and sealing wax—
> Of cabbages—and kings—" (*Dreams*, 147)

Arturo looks at what he has written and "wet [his] lips. It wasn't mine, but what the hell, a man had to start someplace" (*Dreams*, 147). *Dreams from Bunker Hill* concludes with Arturo still struggling to be an author.

Southern California—Fanciful and Absurd

As in much of Fante's fiction, *Dreams from Bunker Hill* pays special attention to architecture. Will Balliett observes that in *Dreams from Bunker Hill* the city is depicted as "both touchingly naive and guilelessly ruthless" (Balliett, 60). The details of two houses in the book—those of Jennifer Lovelace and Velda van der Zee—are especially eloquent articulations of the paradoxically both innocent and contrived nature of Southern California designs.[42] Jennifer Lovelace is the author of "Passion Dawn" (the first manuscript Arturo edits), and her house is as schmaltzy as her story; Arturo describes it as a "wedding cake . . . a yellow and white Victorian fantasy with cupolas at both corners of the second story window. The cupolas were adorned with wood panels of carved spools and intricate patterns of scrolls and twirling figures . . . strangely out of place . . . belonging instead to the Land of Oz" (*Dreams*, 24). Inside the house is a living room of Victorian tenor containing a "grand piano, luxurious chairs, gigantic Boston ferns, Tiffany lamps" (*Dreams*, 25).

Arturo, sensitive to the fairy tale tone of the architecture, declares it a house "out of Mother Goose" (*Dreams*, 24). The design of Jennifer's house recalls not only movie sets but also the expressive abandon (some would say chaos) with which Southern California's architecture is associated.

The decor of Velda van der Zee's house is more overtly Hollywood in that representations of its icons are direct. Pictures of actors predominate: "Every inch of wallspace was crowded with autographed photos of film stars" (*Dreams*, 84). The furniture too is sanctified by the stamp of motion pictures. Velda describes a table as "My favorite desk . . . A Christmas present from Maurice Chevalier," to which the unimpressed Arturo understatedly responds: "It's a beauty" (*Dreams*, 84).

The Pace and Pattern of *Dreams from Bunker Hill*

The pace of *Dreams from Bunker Hill* is brisk, partly due to the steady stream of Arturo's wanderings. Stephen Cooper remarks on these arrivals and departures: "one return leads to another, each as numinous as it is impossible to sustain" (Cooper, 94). Arturo's perpetual uprootings are as much about escapes as they are about searches: on more than one occasion, of course, it is a fistfight or ill-advised seduction that compels Arturo to make a hasty getaway. Still, this uprooting has serious undertones. Arturo, an immigrant to Southern California in self-imposed expatriation, is free to go where he pleases, but he no longer *belongs* anywhere. His unfettered condition is characteristic of the exile and also the writer. If he, in fact, has a home, it is where he is at the novel's end: in front of his typewriter.

What about Art?

When the novel begins, Arturo is enjoying the success of having broken into the short story trade. As with John Fante himself, Arturo went early and straight to the top of the magazine ranks. Soon, however, in terms of prestige, Arturo's writing assignments begin to slip and his connection to his art (short stories) dissolves. He hacks as an editor, a screenwriter, and, perhaps his most comical and lowly position, a very bad poet-for-hire. The fact that Arturo sells out his art for a paycheck is explained by Arturo when he is employed as a screenwriter: "The money kept me there, the absence of poverty, the fear of its return" (*Dreams*, 70).

That Arturo completes almost no "serious" writing during the course of *Dreams from Bunker Hill* is not the unmitigated disaster one might expect from a novel about a young man trying to become an author. In the other Los Angeles novels, Arturo's psyche is painfully engulfed by his pending and then tenuous status as an author as well as his desperate desire to succeed financially. In *Dreams from Bunker Hill,* on the other hand, his fierce personal anxieties about his craft are alleviated by the money in his pockets (until the end, when his pockets are empty). This level of material comfort culminates in a novel that is much less introspective than the other Bandini stories set in Los Angeles. Arturo is still contentious, but his many conflicts hardly send him into the tailspin of self-loathing that they do in *Ask the Dust,* for example.

There are, however, literary disadvantages to Arturo's calmer psyche. One casualty of Arturo's less introspective narration is that Fante's masterful use of euphemistic phrasing and symbolism, though still there, is considerably abbreviated. Elaine Kendall refers to these changes when she writes that *Dreams from Bunker Hill* is "slight in comparison to Fante's earlier Los Angeles novels."[43] Kendall applauds the novel's informal structure as, actually, a productive technique for expanding "upon material that could not be confined within that more rigid form." She also appreciates the novel as a case study of the literary process: "Fante has collected the personal anecdotes that are the novelist's natural resource, showing the reader how fiction is made. Lesser writers merely take these assets away: Fante has sorted and refined them into a finished form" (Kendall, 6).

Dreams from Bunker Hill is a welcome late-date contribution to the Hollywood novels that were being written in the 1930s and 1940s, such as Nathanael West's *Day of the Locust* (1939), F. Scott Fitzgerald's *The Last Tycoon* (1941), and Budd Schulberg's *What Makes Sammy Run?* (1941). *Dreams from Bunker Hill* (1982) was published soon after *Ask the Dust*'s republication and before the other novels were published (or republished, as the case was), and its positive reception makes it therefore entitled to some of the glory of Fante's final fame. Most critics tend to view *Dreams from Bunker Hill* as Kendall does: an informal recollection. However informal it is, *Dreams from Bunker Hill* has its serious side. The novel lucidly reckons with the hero's contending drives between art and money and the choices that conflict produces. When Fante completed *Dreams from Bunker Hill,* the thrills of *Ask the Dust*'s early republication successes were upon him. This newly gained recognition for his literary talents certainly softened the bitterness (bitterness for Hollywood and himself too) he felt toward his decades spent toiling as a screenwriter. This was Fante's last labor of love; in addition to being an entertaining and potent story, it stands as a testament to the peace the author had made with his Hollywood years. Fante's exuberance at revisiting his old haunts, now with a conscience eased of stifling regrets, is evident on every page of *Dreams from Bunker Hill.*

Chapter Four

Fatherhood and Cultural Mediation: *Full of Life; The Brotherhood of the Grape;* "My Dog Stupid"

Full of Life,[1] *The Brotherhood of the Grape,*[2] and the novella "My Dog Stupid"[3] all boisterously highlight the challenges of lives in transition, of growing families and evolving cultural connections. *Full of Life* tells the story of a young married couple in the weeks before the birth of their first child when the paternal grandfather arrives to help fix the house. *The Brotherhood of the Grape* also focuses on the weeks leading up to an event, but here it is a death—that of the same family patriarch, who is going any way but quietly into the dark night. In "My Dog Stupid" an older and rather acerbic author dreams of chucking his family, his responsibilities, and his disappointments for a life in his father's Italy. Out of work and out of patience, he exacts his revenge on the world by adopting an unwanted and ill-mannered dog.

Of the three, *Full of Life*'s is the most jovial treatment of these subjects. Both *The Brotherhood of the Grape* and "My Dog Stupid" are more burly; perhaps they are more brutally honest about the tribulations of growing older and wizened. The principal conflict in all three works centers on a screenwriter protagonist making peace with a querulous Italian father.[4] The protagonists of *The Brotherhood of the Grape* and "My Dog Stupid" struggle with realizing that they themselves have become querulous fathers. The complications of generational schisms during the explosive 1960s give those protagonists a run for their collective money. Money, in fact, is another important issue in these books. The protagonists enjoy a comfortable wealth that contrasts with the embittering poverty in which they were raised. There is no denying that all of the protagonists' lives resemble Fante's own, but it is here that Fante finally calls a text an autobiography. *Full of Life* was sold as a nonfiction representation of Fante's life, and the characters' names mirror those from his life: wife Joyce, father Nick, mother Mary here called Maria. Challenges to the actual veracity of *Full of Life* come not just from his wife but Fante himself. Fante's incorporation of the genre "autobiography," whether literary device, marketing gimmick, or both, entreats a discussion of the autobiographical circumstances of that novel's events.

Full of Life

During Fante's lifetime, *Full of Life* was Fante's most widely admired and best-selling book. He first wrote it as a short story for *Woman's Home Companion* and then expanded it into a novel (Little Brown, 1952). But even before it reached its incarnation as a novel, it earned Fante far and away the most money he had ever seen for a work of literature. In a letter he described to H. L. Mencken the "financial history of this ribald little tome" and concluded that through advances and movie options it earned him "a total of 50 grand for a book that has yet to be put on the market" (*Correspondence*, 136–37). Fante goes on to say that this history proves that "success in this market is a matter of incredible luck" (*Correspondence*, 137). The novel was adapted by Fante for the film *Full of Life*, which was released to acclaim in 1957.[5] Fante was proud of this screenplay, one of his very few produced screenplays that he liked.

Full of Life is a domestic comedy that portrays the impending arrival of a young couple's first child. Taking one of many cues from Fante's real life circumstances, the wife is a college-educated Anglo named "Joyce," and the husband, "John Fante," is an Italian American screenwriter. When the house—a recent acquisition for this nouveau-riche couple—reveals termite damage in the form of a caved-in kitchen floor, the husband brings in his Italian stonemason father (Nick) to fix the problem. John,[6] already harried by his sweet but moody pregnant wife, is forced to suffer embarrassments brought on by his sentimental and unyieldingly Old Country father, not the least of which is the constant stuffing of garlic cloves into keyholes, coin purses, and pockets to ensure that the new grandchild is a son. Meanwhile, wife Joyce has frantic compulsions. Soon, one of these manias includes Catholicism. Though her husband left the religion behind him more than 15 years before, the more Joyce studies it, the more intrigued she becomes. Soon—to the outrage of her husband—she is taking instruction from a priest and preparing to convert. Before long, the interest reveals itself to be more than another obsessional byproduct of pregnancy; it is, in fact, a profound spiritual experience for Joyce. Papa Nick encourages Joyce's conversion, and they conspire against John on other projects too. Nick, brought to Los Angeles to fix the floor, is not at all interested in that task. He wants to give his grandchild a legacy of his stonemason's talent: a gigantic fireplace—something grand enough for Santa Claus to fit through easily. Joyce helps Nick by mixing mortar and carrying stones, two tasks John remembers well from helping his father on worksites as a child. John is constantly buffaloed by father and wife alike—his father refuses to fix the house, his wife refuses to remain the secular pragmatist he married. As the book winds down to its final resolutions, though, the hero meets halfway the challenges to his life: he makes peace with the oversized fireplace and, on the eve of his first child's birth, forges a connection to his Catholic past. In the end, a son is born, and Papa Nick, in a state of euphoria now that his Old World methods for ensuring boys are proven successful, returns home. John and Joyce weather the tribulations of their dramatically changed relationship and start their new lives with greater wisdom and understanding. The only matter unresolved is the kitchen floor: it is never fixed.

The cultural mediations of *Full of Life* are largely conducted via John (the son of an Italian immigrant), Nick (peasant Italy personified), and Joyce (the Anglo wife). The ethnic consciousness of the hero is the most striking shift for Fante's work: generally identified against the powerful bourgeoisie in other novels, the protagonist here is himself quite bourgeois.

Compared to Fante's other works, which tackle ethnic conflicts head-on, *Full of Life* seems uncharacteristically careful and, perhaps, calculatingly so. Fante certainly recognized the marketability of this kind of story in the years following the upheavals of World War II. The United States, a country that fancied itself a nation of immigrants (that is, many nations) was, perhaps ironically, feeling uncertain about cultural and ideological difference. Those concerns were transformed into anxieties about national loyalties. In the late 1940s and early 1950s this fear was institutionalized in the formation of the House Un-American Activities Committee. HUAC was mostly an attempt to flush out Communists and other individuals deemed "un-American"; it conducted hearings where people were questioned about their allegiance to the United States and its democratic principles. For Hollywood these hearings were particularly public. Televised hearings saw well-known and lesser-known actors, directors, and writers questioned about their political and national allegiances. Fante was aware that *Full of Life* was an ideal production opportunity for such a politically charged atmosphere. During that time, Fante wrote to Carey McWilliams about a director called to testify before the committee: "in an effort to prove he had mended his ways [he] declared that one of his future projects was 'Full of Life' by John Fante" (*Letters,* 229). Fante understood the appeal of a politically inoffensive story such as *Full of Life* where difference is, on the surface, reduced to the cultural quirks of a wine-drinking bricklayer from Italy: where difference is, simply, cute.

Critics in the early 1950s recognized that in *Full of Life* Fante was approaching the realm of quaint comedy. Nearly all agreed that it is a sweet story, humorously told, but many also pointed out that the story has serious undertones. P. S. Pasinetti wrote that Fante "must've been so sure of his serious artistic purposes that he daringly liked to work in cliché-ridden territory to prove the freshness of his view. He is very successful in doing so."[7] In his review of the novel, Joseph Henry Jackson explained that *Full of Life* has as much deep wisdom as outward humor: "In short, this is an 'iceberg' book: most of its meaning lies below the surface."[8]

Fante's initial feelings for his most successful novel were enthusiastic, though in later years he denounced it in a letter as "written for money" and "not a very good novel" (*Letters,* 294). But Fante's pride in the novel is indicated in his dedicating it to H. L. Mencken: "This book is for H. L. Mencken with undiminished admiration." Certainly Fante would not have dedicated a book to his mentor if he felt it poorly written. One has to assume that in later years when Fante belittled the accomplishments of *Full of Life* he remembered the book's sweetness and not its weightier themes and the grace of its prose.

The prose in *Full of Life* is surefooted and smooth. Chapters glide into one another with little of the episodic shorthand characteristic of many Fante novels. This is, in part, because the story is not wholly absorbed by the psyche of the protagonist and therefore contains fewer inner-psychic stream of consciousness shifts. *Full of Life* is told by "John Fante," but the spotlight really belongs to wife Joyce and father Nick.

John and Joyce

When the novel opens, John and wife Joyce are luxuriating in their recently acquired wealth. Indeed, much of their lives seems newly acquired—including the house—and a pending acquisition, the birth of their first child, is only weeks away. Though not a best-selling author, John is well paid by Hollywood as a screenwriter. The house is off Wilshire Boulevard in Los Angeles; the home's affiliation with the American success story is in its architectural features: a picket fence, a peaked roof, and a "corridor of rose bushes from the street to the front door, a solid brass knocker on the door" (*Full,* 10). John, still in awe of his success, takes frequent trips out the front door to stand in front and admire his house.

With the newly purchased house and a baby on the way, the relationship between husband and wife is shifting. John thinks back fondly to their early days when his physical passion for her was matched by his need for her intellectual encouragement and insight. He credits Joyce for keeping him a writer: "I was always quitting the craft, hating it, despairing, crumpling paper and throwing it across the room. . . . But she could take the pages and find the good stuff and save it, and plead for more, so that it became habitual with me" (*Full,* 15–16). Now her devotion to her husband's writing has been replaced by her devotion to books on child care.

He sees her drifting from him in other ways too. They occupy separate rooms, so that her restless nighttime activities (walks, trips to the bathroom) do not disturb him. Conversations reflect the lack of dialogue. Alas, poor John is depicted as badgered by his wife.

> She said, "Stop staring."
> She said, "I suppose you spend the whole day looking at slender actresses." (*Full,* 13)

John reacts with unbelievably good humor to the moods and fancies of his gestating Joyce. In many ways, Joyce's pregnancy is clichéd: she is cranky, irrational, given to moodiness. John's responses are also clichéd—he is the put-upon husband fetching sandwiches at unreasonable hours and answering admonishments with "Yes, dear."

Another cliché of Joyce's pregnancy is that she embarks on a series of whirlwind manias. Many of the obsessions bespeak a settling into their new affluence since her behavior vacillates between extravagance and thrift. In one immoderate moment she hires an interior decorator to help her make a decision about drapes. Then, once the drapes have been replaced, she insists on having the furniture recovered to match. Then, in a moment of economy, Joyce fires the housekeeper and starts doing all the housework herself, even washing clothes by hand. That quickly proves unsatisfactory so she rehires the housekeeper. Next, she fires the gardener and personally overhauls the landscaping. During this gardening craze, John describes her hacking out the roses in front and planting bulbs and spending "days crawling under hedges" (*Full,* 14). Each obses-

sion—housework, gardening, eating sandwiches in bed—arrives vigor-
ously and passes quickly.

One of Joyce's enthusiasms, however, does not change except to
increase as the book progresses. This is her growing fascination with
Catholicism, and it marks the unconventional twist to the pregnancy
story. John finds her reading books by "Chesterton and Belloc and
Thomas Merton . . . *The Spirit of Catholicism, The Faith of Our Fathers, The
Idea of a University*" (*Full*, 86). John explains how this interest deviates
radically from his perception of her: "It was incredible to find her with
such books, for she was a cold materialist; she belonged to a semantic
group; nay, she was practically an atheist, with a hard scientific patience
for facts" (*Full*, 86). The "cold materialist" that he married has become,
in a sense, a warm spiritualist. Once she decides to convert, her ultimate
desire becomes to remarry in the church, which would necessitate that
John return to the church too. Her conversion signals another change in
their marriage, for in her journey of theological discovery, Joyce is again
independent from John: he feels no desire to be anything other than the
lapsed Catholic that he is.

Further, Joyce, as an Anglo, university-educated and rather liberated
woman, had represented to John the distance he had come from the
Old-World Italian—in his case—unlettered, traditional world in which
he was raised. His was a deliberate distancing from home and his impatience with his parents' preoccupations (for bearing sons, for instance)
indicates that the desire to keep separate from his given culture remains
strong. It synchronizes a great irony that John's liberated wife would
turn to a Catholicism that to him represents "black shawls" and the Old
World.[9]

John indulges in his own neurotic tendencies. In one scene he convinces himself that the baby has two heads, and that this deformity is
the product of a premarital intimacy: "somewhere in the evil swirl the
penalty had been sown, and now it was time to reap the wicked harvest"
(*Full*, 21).

John has his manias and Joyce has hers. The house, that symbol of
achievement, turns out to be itself unstable. The kitchen floor gives way
under Joyce one morning as she is cooking breakfast, leaving a large
hole in the wooden floor. On further inspection, Joyce finds the entire
floor rotted from fungus and termites. John bangs his heel against the
floor, and "the blow punctured it, leaving a hole" (*Full*, 29). John puts
his ear to the kitchen floor and can hear the noises of the unwelcome
visitors: "Down there, only inches away, I could hear them, the vile

beasts, actually gnawing my wood. It was the rhythmic grinding of thousands of tiny jaws" (*Full*, 32). This act of listening recalls another earlier scene in the first chapter when John listens to the gurgles and splashes of the child inside Joyce. In their ways, the baby and the termites menace John's sense of well-being because they show that his marriage and house are not the fixed, implacable entities he had imagined them. These threats from within the domestic sphere resonate allegorically with the McCarthy era when the nation itself feared the damage that could be done by interlopers.

With his life—wife, self, house—in upheaval, John reaches for an anchor: his father. John reasons that Nick Fante—"the noblest builder of them all!" (*Full*, 32)—is an ideal and inexpensive solution to the ruined floor. An experienced (if flawed) husband and father and an expert builder, Nick Fante represents answers to the very pressing questions in John's life.

Mama and Papa Fante

John travels north to San Juan, near Sacramento, where his parents live, to retrieve his father. The journey north is like a journey into the past, for San Juan is the place where John and Joyce both were raised. Joyce's family is from the "better" side of town—John's is from the proverbial other side of the tracks, "beyond sidewalks and streetlights" (*Full*, 38). The Fante backyard is a slice of pastoral Italy in the Sacramento Valley. Boasting a chicken yard, grapevines, and a garden, with the shade of a fig tree protecting the expanse from the summer sun, the yard indicates how culturally close to Italy Nick and Maria Fante remain.

Almost the same moment that John greets his father in the yard, Nick (who steals every scene) demands to know if his assimilated son has been following the Old Country method for begetting sons. Papa has two granddaughters, but no grandsons, and he insists John do everything in his power to ensure that Joyce has a son. According to Papa, eggs and oysters are the dietary alchemy that guarantees boys. When John mumbles that he thinks that Joyce is carrying a boy, Papa exclaims: "You think! Who asked you to think? I *told* you: oysters. Eggs. I been through it. I give you advice from experience. What you been eating—candy, ice cream? Writer! Bah! You stink like the plague" (*Full*, 41).

Like Papa, Mama is dramatic and John finds greeting his mother the "most difficult task of a homecoming" (*Full*, 41). The humor of her hyperbolic welcome deserves to be quoted at length:

My Mama was the fainting type, specially if we had been away more than three months. Inside three months there was some control over the situation. Then she only teetered dangerously and appeared about to fall over, giving us time to catch her before the collapse. An absence of a month entailed no problem at all. She merely wept for a few moments before the usual barrage of questions. But this was a six-month interval and experience had taught me not to burst in on her. The technique was to enter on tiptoe, put your arms around her from behind, quietly announce yourself, and wait for her knees to buckle. Otherwise she would gasp, "Oh thank God!" and go plummeting to the floor like a stone. Once on the floor she had a trick of sagging in every joint like a mass of quicksilver, and it was impossible to lift her. After futile pawing and grunting on the part of the returned son she got to her feet by her own power and immediately started cooking big dinners. (*Full*, 41)

John, for all his neurotic tendencies, seems a positively stoic fellow in comparison to his parents. Though Nick has dreams of John's returning to San Juan to raise his family and is crestfallen that John has no intention of moving back, Maria eventually convinces her husband to travel to Los Angeles and fix the floor.

The train ride south is hilarious torture for John. Papa immediately ingratiates himself with the porters and passengers who are touched by Papa's peasant simplicity and sentimentality. In what must be punishment for not moving back to San Juan, Nick vilifies his son in between delicate, stagy sips from his jug of wine:

"Children—bah," he muttered.
"Hate their father . . ."
"Better to die. Bury you. Forget you . . ."
"Worked hard all my life . . ."
"Ready to go any time. Done my duty . . ."
"When you're old, they throw you out. . . ." (*Full*, 69–70)

John recounts that his father has his voice "pitched high enough to reach most ears. All around me I felt the smouldering of the others, the heads turning, the shocked stares at me, the pity for my old man" (*Full*, 70). When the dinner bell rings, John is eager for a good meal and he slaps his father on the shoulder: "Come on, Papa. Let's have a nice dinner" (*Full*, 70). But Papa declines with announced self-sacrifice: "I'm all right, son. You go. I don't want to cause you no more trouble. I got my own dinner right here. Try to save you a little money, son" (*Full*, 70). Of course, when John returns from the dining car, Papa is telling everyone the story of his hardscrabble childhood in Abruzzi when he was apprenticed to a cruel stonemason who cheated him of his wages. All the while Nick is telling his "tale of peasant misery" he is carefully eating his "simple repast of bread, cheese, and salami" (*Full*, 71). John feels miserable because he knows that he appears to the passengers to have made his fortune, but also to have betrayed his father: "those near him . . . were deeply moved by the words of this simple old man who found contentment in a bit of bread and cheese and salami while his son gorged himself riotously on rich foods" (*Full*, 72). By the time the train pulls into Los Angeles, everyone is calling Nick "Dad," and no one will speak to John.

Italy Comes to Southern California

When Nick sees his son's home for the first time, his practiced eye ascertains at a glance that the entire house sags in the middle, but he makes no attempt to fix it. Papa has other plans: a desire to leave a legacy to his grandchild. His first gesture in that regard is to insist John transcribe a story of Abruzzi—of Uncle Mingo and the bandits—for his grandchild. John is reluctant: what he really wants is his father to fix the floor and not wallow in sentimental nostalgia. He and his father argue. While at work, John learns that his father has left the house to make his way back to San Juan, too distressed to stay in a house where the story of Uncle Mingo is not appreciated. John finds his father sitting on a bus bench. After promises of a stop at a liquor store (where Nick's desire for a "few" bottles of wine turns into cases delivered to the house later) and a pledge to write down the story of Uncle Mingo, Nick is convinced to return to the house. Resigned to an evening of his father's rambling memories, John sits and shares wine as Papa talks of Abruzzi:

> Uncle Mingo's brother, he was the mayor of Torcelli. We had poor roads in those days. Five thousand people. My cousin Aldo died when he was four . . . Some wheat, but mostly oats . . . Uncle Mingo came over to the house, and he was mad . . . How much can a man stand? You don't know. You sit here in Los Angeles, with plenty to eat, but what do you know about a man's problems? All those rock, falling on his land. The little boy was sick. My mother went over. Wind blowing all the time. The goat died, and Dino went to Rome to be a priest. The taxes were too high. (*Full*, 94–95)

Papa is too connected to the past or too drunk to be able to tell a coherent story of Uncle Mingo and the bandits, but the fragmented memories suggest a time of fearsome poverty and a man who rebelled against his situation. Eventually, an exhausted Papa succumbs to the wine, and John puts him to bed. John stays up for the rest of the night, and out of these "jumbled anecdotes," he coaxes a story. In the morning, pleased with his accomplishment, John brings it downstairs for his father to read: "twenty good pages about an Italian bandit, a heroic figure with red hair" (*Full*, 97). Papa, however, is not interested in reading the story: "What I got to read it for? Good God, kid, I lived it" (*Full*, 97).

The inscription of an Italian story for a later generation echoes notions of cultural connection for the children of immigrants as discussed by many critics.[10] According to this archetype, the first generation stays invested in the home country, the second generation comes to identify more with the adopted country (thereby undergoing assimilation), and the third generation develops a fascination for the home country's traditions, traditions from which the previous generation had distanced itself. In *Full of Life* the telling of the story of Uncle Mingo encapsulates this generational trajectory. Nick's story of Uncle Mingo (Italy) skips over the second generation's disinterest (John, the assimilated son, is not receptive to writing the story) to await the certain fascination of the third generation (the child to be born).

The second legacy that Papa wants to leave to his grandchild is the grand fireplace noted earlier. It is huge, belonging more to a mountain chalet than a suburban Southern California house, but it was not, after all, built out of necessity, but out of Nick's egotism and theatrical love.

The conflicts in the novel are nearly all resolved at the book's end. A baby, a son, is born. Nick forgives John for not coming back to San Juan. Joyce forgives John for not returning with her to the church. John forgives Joyce for turning to the church. Finally, as Joyce is in labor, John happens upon a chapel and prays for his wife, himself, and their baby and thereby makes a significant and heartfelt connection to the church. John and Joyce's marriage is reaffirmed and fortified by the birth of Nick, named for his paternal grandfather (the custom for the first son). The hole in the kitchen floor remains; Nick tells John to call a carpenter to fix it.

Gender

Full of Life marks one of the few times that Fante gives a leading female character a realistic complexity.[11] Initially, Joyce is depicted in a comical light, hiring and firing—with equal rapidity—the "hired help." In one scene she unreasonably insists on sharing John's single bed though her pregnant form makes their simultaneous occupation of the bed physically impossible. Even her conversion to Catholicism is described by her husband as rather silly. After she decides to convert, one of her main difficulties is trying to select a patron saint. John suggests Saint Teresa: "She's got a big reputation, all over the world" (*Full*, 101). Joyce responds: "Too popular . . . Not obscure, not mysterious enough. Besides, she was an awfully plain woman. Personally I lean toward Saint Elizabeth. She was very rich and very beautiful. She wrote well, too. I feel very close to Saint Elizabeth. I think she understands me better than anyone in the world." John ridicules her analysis, but her sense of spiritual empowerment makes her impervious to his sarcasm: "I'm ready for your scoffs . . . You're in my prayers constantly" (*Full*, 101). Her rather silly sanctimoniousness subsides as her conversion date (and the date of the birth of their baby) approaches.

In addition to Joyce's frenzies, John reports too her newfound strength: "She was very pretty, with gray eyes incredibly bright. Something new was added to those eyes. Fearlessness. It was startling. You looked away" (*Full*, 11). The self-assurance that he sees in her acknowledges the profundity of her experience. Later, when she is baptized, John is struck by Joyce's deep happiness saying it was "almost terrifying. As [the priest] read the ritual, first in Latin, then in English, the tears ran freely down her cheeks. . . . Hers was a shattering kind of happiness" (*Full*, 137).

Characters and Caricatures

In many ways, the characters in *Full of Life* are exaggerated. Papa Nick, Joyce, Maria, John himself, and even Joyce's priest are all histrionic and emotionally unabashed throughout the book: they weep, they shout, they say how they feel. Rose Basile Green saw this as symptomatic of Fante's work and rather dismissively refers to it as "out of place emotionalism."[12] One 1952 reviewer commented on this aspect of the novel when she observed that "not everybody could live on that level of emotional velocity, but the Fantes seem built for it."[13] Certainly the effect of these exaggerated emotions and characters is outrageous and often comical. But the novel is kept from broad farce because it is built on the foundation of the serious feelings that compel these heightened emotions. Maria, for instance, is melodramatic, in varying degrees, when her children return home: her behavior ranges from the loud exclamation, to the hand-to-the-forehead swoon, and finally the total collapse on the floor. For John, his mother's fainting is ridiculous and tiresome, but also terrifying and not just because it is difficult to determine an actual from a fake heart attack. Part of what is so terrifying is that seeing her children again really does overwhelm Maria to the point of passing out (Jackson, 20). Maria's is a terrifying love for John because it so debilitates her; he, of course, is on the verge of being a parent and perhaps frightened to imagine himself loving something (here, a child) so much.

In the characterization of Joyce too there is near caricaturization, but this is balanced by sincere and noble feeling. Her interactions with Catholic dogma strike John as humorous, particularly in that her debate over selecting a patron saint is reduced to choosing between the plain and popular one or the obscure and pretty one. But in spite of those absurdities, there is a formidable conversion taking place before John's eyes. And though he cannot share his wife's passion in this, John marvels at the strength of her feeling when he accompanies her to church: "And yet I could sit beside her before the altar, her small hands exquisite in green kid gloves, and I could adore her for the beauty of her effort, the striving of her heart, the mighty force that prompted her to be but a good woman, humble and grateful before God" (*Full,* 136).

Autobiographical Elements of *Full of Life*

Because *Full of Life* makes so many explicit gestures to John Fante's real life, the autobiographical elements of the novel warrant comment.

It was Fante's editors who suggested he use real names and call this book nonfiction. This Fante did, though in a letter to Mencken he acknowledged the story was "fiction, pure and simple" (*Correspondence,* 137). Reviewers in 1952 and in 1988, when Black Sparrow Press republished it, presumed the story's veracity. And why not: the protagonist identifies himself in the opening pages as "John Fante, composer of books" (*Full,* 11).

Joyce Fante describes the time during which Fante was writing the novel as the "polar opposite of the sunny domestic scene" depicted in the novel (*Letters,* 225). Fante, according to his wife, was gambling or golfing almost full time. Domestic tensions were exacerbated with arguments over the size their family would take. At the time *Full of Life* was written, Fante was a father of three, and another son was on the way.

Joyce Fante has also discussed her conversion to Catholicism, which was actual but, according to her, motivated not by metaphysical need, but practical interest. In an interview she says: "When Nick [the eldest son] got to be school age, I had to take instructions from the church because we were sending him to a Catholic school. So the priest converted me" ("Interview"). She was enthusiastic about joining the church and the reasons why are amusing: "I love tests. [The priest] had a little book with a test at the end of every chapter. And I was so proud of myself for passing all these tests that I got really enthusiastic about the Catholic church and joined. Having studied English [in college], I'd read the *Faerie Quene* so I wasn't unacquainted with the Seven Deadly Sins" ("Interview"). It is noteworthy that Fante, who has sometimes been accused of making light of serious life, here turned the light circumstances of his wife's conversion into a serious event.

Joyce Fante attests to the actuality of an Uncle Mingo too: "There was an Uncle Mingo. He had red hair and was a bandit and they [the Fantes] were all very proud of him" ("Interview").

As noted before, *Full of Life* was successful as a story, an abridged novel (in *Reader's Digest*), a novel, and, finally, as a film. Fante's screenplay for *Full of Life* was not the only personal contribution made to the film. In an incident of life becoming art, his Italian relatives lent pictures and wall decorations that were used in the movie ("Interview").

In 1952 the book was reviewed widely and enthusiastically.[14] Its republication in 1988 also inspired a number of reviews, but the novel struck many as dated.[15] The subject matter of *Full of Life* is pretty wholesome; that conservatism grates on the nerves of today's critics. Geoffrey Dunn sees in the novel a resemblance to the television show "Father Knows Best."[16] As noted, *Full of Life*'s relatively unrisky handling of ethnicity contrasts sharply to Fante's other novels. Lionel Rolfe asked writer Gerald Locklin about this variance—from reckless to safe—in Fante's writing. Locklin sees the early works as "a little nastier, more self-revealing."[17] Locklin goes on to judge that Hollywood's quick fix, happily-ever-after tendencies had infected Fante's work from all his years writing scripts: "there's a slickness, strictly Bad News Bears, in some of his later works" (Rolfe, 35).[18] It is, however, important to remember that humor and happy endings are the distinguishing characteristics of comedy, and a comedy is what this novel unequivocally is. Fante's natural tendency was to fold tragedy into the mix, but in *Full of Life* he sustains the comedy throughout the novel. The serious undertones of religion, fatherhood, and cultural mediation are present, but the challenges they pose ultimately do not threaten the happiness of "Joyce" and "John Fante." One recent critic had a more forgiving reaction to *Full of Life*. Brooke K. Horvath enthuses that the novel's touching sentiment never quite becomes sentimental and that "today it will seem a terribly unfashionable novel, which is too bad for us."[19]

The success of his *Full of Life* screenplay helped keep Fante a sought-after screenwriter for years. During those years of screenwriting, Fante began longer works such as *1933 Was a Bad Year* and "My Dog Stupid," but screenwriting effectively supplanted Fante's literary writing for a quarter century. His 1977 novel, *The Brotherhood of the Grape*, would tell a wholly different kind of story about family and fatherhood.

The Brotherhood of the Grape

As in *Full of Life*, the screenwriter protagonist of *The Brotherhood of the Grape* goes home to his Italian parents; this time it is not to bring his father to Los Angeles, but rather to ensure that he stays up north. After 51 years of marriage, his parents are threatening to divorce. Nick Molise, stonemason, patriarch, and family baddie, remains a tyrant though ill and 76 years old. When son Henry arrives on the scene, he faces an unexpected challenge: his father needs a helper on a job. The trip home becomes an opportunity for Henry, now a 50-year-old father of two himself, to repair the schismed relationship between he and his father and to prepare for the older man's death. The events' sense of finality, of these characters taking their last stand in their idiosyncratic ways, gives the book a power both touching and convincing.

The Brotherhood of the Grape (1977) marked Fante's return to sustained fiction; it was the first novel he had published in the 25 years since *Full of Life*. Screenwriting assignments were increasingly scarce for Fante in the late 1960s, and certainly that paucity of work compelled him to find his creative outlet in his fiction. He had dabbled with novel ideas after *Full of Life* and, in fact, Fante described a story about his father's last days in a letter to a prospective editor as early as 1954 (*Letters*, 231). With his own health in decline, there has been speculation that Fante wrote this book to reckon not only with the 1950 death of his father but also his own.[20] From whatever motivation, this return to novels proved a joyous one for Fante. While writing the novel, Fante wrote to McWilliams that it was "by far my best work" (*Letters*, 297). The writing of the book was an emotional project. Fante later said about it: "It was the one book I took a tremendous joy in writing . . . My phrasing sometimes pleased me very much. Sometimes I thought I was brilliant. Sometimes I cried when I wrote that book."[21]

When the novel was published it was reviewed not widely, but well. Fante's portrayal of the emotionally volatile Molise family drew especially positive notices. Joe David Bellamy of the *New York Times Book Review* commented that the antics of the Molises are "so excessive, one wonders that they don't *seem* made up; yet the sense of verisimilitude . . . is unwavering, and its action compelling".[22] In Carolyn See's *Los Angeles Times* review, she lauded the book as another one of Fante's "extremely weird and interesting" novels.[23]

The Brotherhood of the Grape is dense with colorful characterizations and subplots.[24] The book's forthright tone sharpens the characters' actions, which can be unappealing when not altogether repellent. The sex in the novel, for instance, leans more toward expressions of desperation than love or even lust. Papa Nick is not above using his fists against his wife and sons. The novel's visceral candor is seen in the emotions of its characters, and their strength of passion—in love and in anger—is awesome. The family's winsome moments seen in *Full of Life* have disappeared these many years hence. Their grudges are flanked by disappointments and frustrations decades old. Loyalties are deep too, however. The book's most pleasurably sensuous scenes take place in Mama Molise's kitchen, where her never-wavering love is clearly expressed through the feasts she prepares for her children.

When the novel begins, 50-year-old Henry Molise, the book's narrator, is the not-so-proud possessor of two sons (both in their early 20s, and mostly on their own), a wife (Harriet, whose wisdom makes her more a rival than a lover), a mortgage, a dormant screenwriting career, and a past-due novel he cannot seem to complete. Though his sons are only a minor focus of the novel, knowing Henry is a father himself adds complexity to his dealings with his own father. In his Southern California beach house, Henry lives in bourgeois comfort, addled but flush with the distance he has achieved from the poverty of his childhood. His Italian American mother, Italian father, and siblings live a secure distance away, near Sacramento in San Elmo.[25] But a phone call brings Henry's primary and acquired worlds crashing together and returns him to his origins, where the conflicts of old are alive and, unfortunately, well.

Youngest brother Mario calls to report the most recent fight between their parents. Maria, a woman who thought her worries about her husband's wandering ways were long over, found a pair of Papa's underpants besmirched with the lipstick of some *puttana*. She confronts him with the evidence, the fight escalates until Nick grasps his wife by the throat and kicks her backside. At that moment, Mario stops by for a visit, and Nick retreats out the door, ashamed of himself. The police are called, Nick is jailed (the sheriff is a fellow Elk, so the incarceration is pretty friendly), Mama drops the charges, and as soon as he is out of jail, Papa goes after Mario on the street in front of the courthouse. Mario ends up with a broken nose, not the first blow he has received from his father. People gather to watch the fight, and Maria tells the shocked crowd about the wicked underwear. Mario and the other siblings who live in San Elmo (Stella and Virgil and their spouses) are humiliated by the public display. Bruises remain on Maria the next day (as unmistakable as the guilty lipstick), and she shouts to the rooftops that she is finally fed up and wants a divorce. Although the siblings are concerned about their mother's ill-treatment, they are clearly more concerned about what their parents' divorce could mean to them. Tired of coping with the pair of them, Mario insists that Henry come home to save their parents' marriage. Henry knows that in the event of a divorce, he would have to take one of them in—perhaps, God forbid, his father—and that realization convinces him to act on his brother's desperate request for help and go home to do what he can to salvage the marriage.

Once Henry arrives in San Elmo, the immediate crisis has blown over. When Henry broaches the subject to his mother, she laughs: "We're Catholics, we can't divorce. Didn't you know that?" (*Brotherhood,* 48). His parents are still, metaphorically, at each other's throats, but the reader quickly learns that this state of affairs is status quo. Indeed, Henry and his siblings have negotiated peace settlements between Nick and Maria before.

Nick and his Brotherhood at the Café Roma

Though his parents' relationship is the same, Henry sees big changes in his father. Of Fante's patriarchs, this Nick Molise is the most bad tempered; less the cheeky scamp of *Full of Life* or *1933 Was a Bad Year,* in *The Brotherhood of the Grape,* the father is a menace and a brute. Once indomitable (and obviously still a bully) Nick is physically fading: "the patina of vitality was gone from his movements. He had lost weight and the seat of his khaki trousers drooped sadly" (*Brotherhood,* 33). Henry sees the years in Nick's eyes: "Their sparkle was gone, as if behind a yellowish film and a net of small red veins" (*Brotherhood,* 42).

These days, Nick spends most of his time with his cronies, the eponymous brotherhood of the grape, at the Café Roma, a headquarters for the male Italian community, that features a makeshift brothel upstairs. The Café Roma's clientele has always been old Italian men, but in the years since Henry was a kid there have been changes. Henry thinks, "The old men I remembered were planted in the graveyard, replaced by a new generation of old men" (*Brotherhood*, 39). Henry sees that the once-favored language of the café, Italian, has been replaced by English. An Italian flag remains on the café wall, but it is fly specked and dusty. Newer is a gilt-framed poster of Marlon Brando in *The Godfather*, in what seems like an expression of Italy by way of Hollywood—a kind of refracted and filtered symbol of Italian pride.

The waning of the Café Roma's homegrown Italianitá is correlated with the passing of generations, from first generation immigrants to later, more assimilated generations. But the passing of this generation is not wrapped in a soft shawl of nostalgia for Italy. Henry describes the old men in the bar as "a cranky, irascible, bitter gang of Social Security guys, intense, snarling, rather mean old bastards . . . enjoying their cruel wit, their profanity and their companionship" (*Brotherhood*, 39). "Simply old men killing time, waiting for the clock to run down," is how Henry assesses them, but he is startled to realize that his father is now one of these old men.

Italy Is in the Kitchen

One place where Italian culture is flourishing is in Mama's kitchen. The two sons who live in San Elmo often visit solely for the food, neither of their Anglo wives having adopted Italian cooking. The strong evocations of the kitchen's scents and its old-world enticements are detailed in one long sentence:

> the true mother country, this warm cave of the good witch deep in the desolate land of loneliness, with pots of sweet potions bubbling over the fire, a cavern of magic herbs, rosemary and thyme and sage and oregano . . . this small twenty-by-twenty world, the altar a kitchen range, the magic circle a checkered tablecloth where the children fed, the old children, lured back to their beginnings, the taste of mother's milk still haunting their memories, eyes brightening, the wicked world receding as the old mother witch sheltered her brood from the wolves outside. (*Brotherhood*, 55)

During one meal the power of the food overwhelms Henry to the point of crying: "The gnocchi prepared in butter and milk finally did it. I covered my eyes over the plate and wept with joy, sopping my tears with a napkin" (*Brotherhood*, 51).

Maria's cooking is an expression of her deep maternal love, but it also serves a diplomatic function: it leavens the perpetual unpleasantness between Nick and his children. For instance, after Henry and his father have an argument at the Café Roma, Henry stomps home. As he gets closer to the house and smells the "ambrosial waft of sweet basil" emanating from the kitchen, the "ugly scene" vanishes from his mind (*Brotherhood*, 46). But Maria's culinary devotions, delivered to Henry on this visit home, mask a barbed hook. Nick and Maria are conspiring to keep Henry in town as long as possible.

The conspiracy becomes evident immediately upon Henry's hasty arrival in San Elmo. With the divorce no longer a threat, Papa's thoughts turn to a new job. Nick has agreed to build a stone smoke-house up in the mountains, at the motel of his friend Sam Ramponi (another member of the brotherhood). With his former hod carriers deceased or too old, Nick reasons that this is a good opportunity for Henry: "Easy job. Little stone house . . . Ten by ten. No windows. One door. I'll lay up the walls, you mix the mortar, carry the stone. Nice place. Good country. Forest. Big trees. Mountain air. Do you good . . . I pay ten dollars a day. Board and room. Seven days a week. We'll be outa there in two weeks if you don't waste time or quit on me. You want the job? You got it. But remember who's boss. I do the thinkin" (*Brotherhood*, 42). Not surprisingly, Henry is not enthusiastic about the job offer and, initially, he refuses to consider it. Not only do his father's tyrannical tendencies make being in his employ unappealing, the offer itself reignites old grudges: Nick, after all, refuses to acknowledge the legitimacy of the profession Henry has chosen. When Henry protests that he cannot stay in San Elmo because of the book he has to finish, Nick scoffs: "Book! You call that work?" (*Brotherhood*, 36).

Work

The characterization of Nick Molise is consistent with Fante's other descriptions of patriarchs who have similar predilections for philandery, wine, and gambling. Fante's patriarchs are also craftsmen, and Nick Molise is particularly exceptional. Henry remembers his father dragging him and his brothers through San Elmo on what they called the "Grand Tour, the complete works of Nick Molise" (*Brotherhood*, 20). Though suited-up and nearly late already for a high school baseball game, Henry remembers an evening when his father took him on the tour. In front of the public library, Nick stops, awed by his own art. Henry recalls:

> Pausing across the street, hands on hips, [Nick's] face softened reverently as he stared at the building.
> "There she is, kid. Isn't she pretty? You know who built her?"
> "You did, Papa."
> "Not bad. Not bad at all."
> "Last a thousand years."
> "At least."
> "Look at that stone, those steps. They flow like water." (*Brotherhood*, 21)

Henry cannot hide his admiration for his father's skill as he ticks off the buildings his father created: "The City Hall. The Bank of California. Municipal Water and Power, Spanish-style with adobe colonnades and a red tile roof. Haley's Mortuary. The Criterion Theatre. The Fire Department, all red brick and spotless, with expanses of flawless concrete" (*Brotherhood*, 21).

But along with Henry's reverence for Nick's worthy talents boil the concurrent memories of his selfishness. Henry recalls the rage he felt about his family's "poverty in the midst of my father's prosperity" (*Brotherhood*, 81), for though his father earned good wages, the money went to his own vices: the family was barely given enough for basic groceries or other bills. Henry ruminates on his father's disinterested and irresponsible parenting: "My old man had never wanted children. He had wanted apprentice bricklayers and stonemasons. He got a writer, a bank teller, a married daughter, and a railroad brakeman. In a sense he tried to shape his sons the way he shaped stone, by whacking it. He failed, of course, for the more he hammered at us, the further he drove us from any love for the craft" (*Brotherhood*, 25).

Mario and Bricks and Baseball

The youngest son, Mario, had tried to take up stonemasonry, but Nick was a merciless boss, making him perform often meaningless tasks (to break him down and build him up again). Nick paid his son very little and "only when the spirit moved him. He felt that Mario should actually be working for nothing, just for the privilege of having such an illustrious maestro" (*Brotherhood*, 26–27). Three months into this thankless apprenticeship (set to last for seven years), Mario is recruited as a pitcher by a professional baseball team (the San Francisco Seals, in the Pacific Coast League). The family is thrilled for Mario, but Nick is adamantly against the idea: "baseball was a foolish way to earn a living. . . . Better that [Mario] should have an honorable profession, that of a stonemason, building with brick and stone" (*Brotherhood*, 26).[26] Since Mario is not yet 18 and the team needs parental consent, Nick has his way and Mario returns to breaking rocks and lugging stones. After Mario turns 18 and hears that the baseball deal is off (by then the major league had moved west, supplanting the Pacific Coast League), he walks off the job. Mario settles for semiprofessional baseball, pitching in Sacramento Valley cities. Nick is enraged by Mario's defection from bricklaying: "He sold me out . . . He deserted his own father" (*Brotherhood*, 27). In retaliation, Nick faithfully attends Mario's baseball games, but only to heckle his son and encourage opposing batters: "Knock him out of there! Knock his brains out!" (*Brotherhood*, 27). At a playoff game, when Mario hits a home run to win a league championship game, Nick actually runs out of the stands and onto the field to tackle his youngest son as he rounds third base.

Nick and Writing

Nick is similarly disgusted with Henry's lack of interest in stonemasonry. Even more distressing for Nick is that in the years after high school, Henry becomes fascinated with books. This literary interest and the consequent distancing that develops between father and son echoes the alienation effect that Thomas Ferraro characterizes for authors from immigrant homes.[27] Henry remembers his growing devotion to the written word: "Trapped and barricaded against the darkness and the loneliness of the valley, I used to sit with library books piled on the kitchen table, desolate, listening to the call of the voices in the books, hungering for other towns" (*Brotherhood*, 60). Nick tries to stop Henry's constant reading by berating his son: "Get out of here! There's a war on. Get in the army . . . Support yourself. Be a man. You know what a man is? A man works. He sweats. He digs. He pounds. He builds" (*Brotherhood*, 61). The rift between father and eldest son increases until they are barely speaking at home or in public. Henry recalls one day when they pass each other in the street, Nick pretending to be reading a book while laughing and pointing at Henry. Henry's taking up of writing is in some ways more threatening to Nick than Mario's defection, because authorship takes place far from the Sacramento Valley, in a world beyond the stonemason's reach. Henry is not vulnerable to Nick in the same way as his brother, Mario, because there is no public forum—no baseball field—on which Nick can tackle his author son.

In spite of his father's ridicule and disapproval, the young Henry reads on. Henry remains frustrated with his family circumstances until the day he reads Dostoyevsky for the first time: "he spoke to me of man and the world, of love and wisdom, pain and guilt, and I knew I would never be the same . . . he knew more about fathers and sons than any man in the world . . . I found I could breathe, could see invisible horizons. The hatred for my father melted. I loved my father, poor, suffering, haunted wretch" (*Brotherhood*, 62). Reading Dostoyevsky inspires in Henry an empathy for his father, who he had earlier declared a "streetcorner Dago . . . low-born Abruzzian wop . . . yahoo peasant" (*Brotherhood*, 61). In fact, Dostoyevsky so moves Henry that he decides that he wants to be a writer himself. In this epiphanic moment Henry feels a simultaneous pull toward and away from his father. On the one hand, Dostoyevsky inspires him to leave home and go out into the world and write (this is a path away from his hometown and, in effect, his father). On the other hand, Dostoyevsky transforms Henry's anger at his father into empathy and love (a method for being close to his father). By conceptualizing his father and his life in terms of the poetics of a story, Henry perceives his maddening father with love and understanding. His desire to write operates as an homage, in many ways, to Henry's desire to be close to his father.

Now a professional author, Henry does not regret his decision to forego stonemasonry. But the desire to please his father remains strong—stronger, in fact, than his desire to *not* work for his father. He thinks that not helping his father build this smokehouse might "bring a swifter death," and he does not want "that shadow over the rest of [his] life" (*Brotherhood*, 82). He decides to assist Nick, for, Henry reasons, the old man "was entitled to this last paltry triumph, this little house of stone in the Sierras" (*Brotherhood*, 82). Moreover, working for his father seems fated, unavoidable. Henry thinks: "So it had come down to this. I was a hod carrier at long last" (*Brotherhood*, 78).

Before heading up to the mountains to perform his duty as a son, he has to perform his duty as a husband. At Harriet's vehement insistence, Henry pays a visit to his mother-in-law. Hilda Dietrich lives in a "jewel box" of a house on the aristocratic side of San Elmo, the house and grounds of which are as meticulously tended as her hatred for her Italian American son-in-law. Hilda is characterized as thoroughly and malevolently Anglocentric, and she functions in the novel as a reminder of the ethnic conflicts Henry faced growing up in San Elmo. Hilda's initial distrust of him is fueled by a belief that, as an Italian, he would naturally be armed. When courting, Henry and Harriet were forced to rendezvous out of town, to avoid her disapproving and forbidding eye. Finally, they eloped. Hilda's continued dislike for him is evident in her calling him neither by his first name nor his proper last name: she refers to him as "Mr. Malice."

The interlude with Hilda Dietrich is brisk and bitter. When he returns to his inherited side of town, Nick and two members of the brotherhood have loaded the truck with beer and tools and are awaiting Henry's return.

They take to the road: the older men in the truck's cab sing and toss back beer; Henry in the truck camper (with the wheelbarrow) sipping a beer and watching the "lovely autumn hillsides glid[e] by, the manzanita, the scrub oaks and pine, the farmhouses, the vineyards, cattle and sheep grazing among white stones, the peach and pear orchards" (*Brotherhood*, 92). They stop at Angelo Musso's vineyard. Angelo is their preferred vintner and his wine (the brotherhood's lifeblood) is delivered to their doorsteps monthly in gallon jugs.

The Winery

The trip they make to the vineyard is described like a pilgrimage to a divine site. The men kiss with reverence the hand of the aged Angelo Musso, who reposes at a table under the grape arbor. He nods in acknowledgment of their arrival, but says nothing (cancer having taken his larynx years before). Henry describes most of the "old-time Italians in Placer County" as looking to Angelo for advice, though he cannot speak; seekers read solutions to their problems in Angelo's posture, his yellowish eyes, and his silence. This oracular aspect of Angelo connects to the atmosphere of classical mythology that characterizes the Musso vineyard overall. Angelo's housekeeper, Odette, brings the assembled brotherhood jugs of wine and trays of bread and homemade mozzarella; the visitors gorge while tossing kisses Angelo's way to show their pleasure and respect (*Brotherhood*, 95). The bees, omnipresent with the grapevines, buzz around and form a "little halo around Angelo's gray hair and helped themselves to his cheese and wine" (*Brotherhood*, 95). Though his quiet passivity would not seem to inspire it, Angelo presides over what effectively becomes an afternoon Dionysian orgy. Henry says: "We got down to deep meditative drinking, the witchery of the wine transcending the miracle of its taste, enveloping our souls within the cocoon of the humming bees . . . Hypnos descended and time passed to the drone of the bees" (*Brotherhood*, 96). When Henry awakens, his hung-over eyes behold the surroundings after the debauch. One of his father's friends is lurching out of the winery doors with Odette in tow. Odette sees Henry and offers him "action." Henry retreats, alighting for the dis-tant sprinklers in a field where he peels off his clothes and stands beneath the purifying spray. When Henry returns, he sees his father stumbling out the winery doors with Odette. Disgusted, Henry loads his father into the truck and delivers a kick to the old man's rear, per-haps in retaliation for the kick Nick delivered to Maria earlier.

On the Mountain

Finally, Henry manages to get the old men back in the truck and up to the mountain motel. The next day, when it is time to work, Nick assumes the posture of dictator that Henry remembers detesting when he was a kid. Nick "barks" at his (50-year-old) son: "You, boy! Get this here truck unloaded" (*Brotherhood*, 101). Henry responds with a sarcastic salute and a crisp: "Right on, sir!" But while working for his father remains the same, his father's abilities have lessened dramatically. Though Nick insists on toughing it out, the strain of placing heavy stones overwhelms him so that he has to sit down every few minutes. By the end of the day, Nick's back is out of alignment, and he has to eat his lunch lying on his stomach near the mountain creek. Henry remembers his father's glory years, when his father built churches and schools, "but now he was having a hell of a time putting up a ten-foot smokehouse" (*Brotherhood*, 115).[28]

More remarkable than Nick's obvious physical vulnerabilities are his emotional vulnerabilities. After a night spent drinking and playing cards with his friends, Nick passes out cold in the motel room he shares with Henry, but he does not sleep peacefully. He sobs for his mother, dead in Italy for 60 years: "Mama mia, mama mia" (*Brotherhood*, 107). Nick's cries for his mother torment Henry, and the son comforts his father: "I gathered his limp head in my arms. . . . I wiped his tears with a corner of the sheet, I rocked him like a child, and soon he was no longer crying, and I eased him gently to the pillow and he slept quietly" (*Brotherhood*, 108). Henry is able to be kind, even maternal, to his father, but his sympathy for his father clearly distresses him. Henry can cope with an irascible father, but being nice to a weeping father is a new and unpleasant development. Based on Nick's historic brutality, Henry feels that his father hardly deserves love. In the morning, Nick has no recollection of his crying and he returns to being the loutish foreman. After a couple of tense days working together on the smokehouse, Nick and Henry achieve a companionable relationship. Molise and son finish the job, and in so doing, build a physical symbol of the bond between them.[29] The work pace accelerates in time with the drinking and increasing goodwill. In contradistinction to his former strict building methods, Nick gives into the wine, tosses "aside the plumb line . . . [and] works by instinct. . . . The wall went up and the wine went down" (Brotherhood, 118). In fact, the structure is more slapdash sculpture than orderly building: "The stones appeared to have been thrown into the wall rather than set. The walls waved crazily, convex and concave. . . . Mortar oozed from the joints" (Brotherhood, 121). Probably, Henry could have built it himself. The night after Nick and Henry finish the job, a tremendous rainstorm returns the crooked smokehouse to its original state: a pile of rocks. Though Henry is amused at the rubble, when Nick sees it in the morning he is appalled. Nick wants to build it again, correctly, and so begins to wrestle with the stones. Before the morning is done, Nick collapses next to the smokehouse ruins.

This is a pivotal moment in the novel. What had seemed like geriatric high jinks and the effects of bad hangovers now appears to have been the symptoms of grave illness. At the hospital, Nick is roused from the diabetic coma he was in.[30] The family physician informs Henry that his father has many health problems, all of which Nick had insisted on not communicating to his family. The physician informs Henry that the diabetes will kill Nick if he does not severely restrict his sugar intake and cut back on pasta, bread, and wine—the staples of Nick's diet.

Initially, Nick is a perfect penitent patient. When asked how he feels, he says: " 'Nice place. Nurses, nice. . . . I feel good,' he said. Then, pleased: 'I take insulin now' " (Brotherhood, 149). One advantage to the hospital stay is his blond nurse, Miss Quinlan, who calls a thrilled Nick her "naughty little boy" (Brotherhood, 150). Nick at first makes his peace with his new circumstances and new life: "Lots to learn . . . What I eat, what I can't eat. Not like the old days. No more pasta. Not much, anyway." Maria is astonished that pasta could ever be a culprit: "No pasta . . . no spaghetti?" (Brotherhood, 149). Maria's skepticism seems to doom Nick's new health-consciousness. Nick bypasses the certain, if delicious, death that awaits him in his wife's kitchen. After two days in the hospital, when his return home seems imminent, he calls the brotherhood of the grape; they spring him from the hospital.

The Winery, Redux

Henry is initially amused at his father's escape, but when he learns how desperately his father needs insulin, he searches every likely bar for Nick. Finally, he drives to Angelo Musso's winery where he finds his father resting at a table under the grape arbor, surrounded by his friends, Angelo Musso, and a half-eaten feast of wine and bread. The classical imagery continues: "Drooping majestically, my old man slumped deep in a wicker chair, hopelessly drunk, his arms limp over the chair arms. He was like an ancient Roman patrician waiting for the blood to drain from his slitted wrists" (*Brotherhood*, 158). Henry wants to return his father to the hospital, but when he attempts to move the old man, the brotherhood voices its protest. Angelo, the mute sage, writes notes to Henry that the younger man needs translated from Italian: "It is better to die of drink than to die of thirst" and "It is better to die among friends than to live among doctors" (*Brotherhood*, 160). The aphorisms draw tears from Henry, who knows that he is watching his father die, but elicit applause from the men at table: "a clapping of hands, glasses held aloft and drained in a toast, even a wave from my father, who was beyond the point of understanding anything" (*Brotherhood*, 160). An ambulance (called by the family doctor) soon arrives to wrangle Nick back to the hospital. As the attendants put Nick on a stretcher, the brotherhood murmur their farewells in Italian:

> "Ciao, Nicola, Buono fortuna."
> "Addio, amico mio."
> "*Corragio*, Nick."
> "Corragioso, Nicola." (*Brotherhood*, 161)[31]

Nick dies on the way to the hospital.

The day before his father's funeral, Henry pays a visit to the public library, built by his father long before. He makes his way through the stacks to that "familiar place in the corner by the window near the pencil sharpener below the portrait of Mark Twain, and drew out the leather-bound copy of *The Brothers Karamazov*" (*Brotherhood*, 171). With a tenderness he could never have shown his father, Henry embraces the book: "I held it in my hands, I leafed the pages, I drew it tightly into my

arms, my life, my joy, my sublime Dostoyevsky. I may have failed him in
my deeds, but never in my devotion. My beloved Papa was gone, but
Fyodor Mikhailovich would be with me to the end of my life" (*Brotherhood,* 171).

Mama is rather relieved to have Papa dead, for she can now be sure of
his whereabouts and his fidelity. She copes with her grief by feeding her
children. In the final lines of the novel, as the family walks from Papa's
grave, Mama is already planning the family meal, down to the side
dishes: " 'I bought a leg of lamb,' she said. 'We'll have a nice dinner. The
whole family. With new potatoes' " (*Brotherhood,* 178).

In this novel Fante takes off the gloves in presenting the throes of a
difficult family life and an especially trying father. The narrative is shorn
of niceties, but rich with energy and wit. This is Fante's most dense
book and there is a sense that settling scores with his father was a formidable task.

Ultimately, *The Brotherhood of the Grape* puts to rest the Italian father
who had antagonized Fante and his protagonists for decades.[32]

"My Dog Stupid"

In contrast to *The Brotherhood of the Grape,* where an assimilated son is
largely distanced from his Italian past, in "My Dog Stupid" the assimilated son identifies strongly with his Italian background. For Henry
Molise (note the same name as in *Brotherhood*) in "My Dog Stupid," Italian culture captivates and anchors the assimilated protagonist.

Fante wrote "My Dog Stupid" in the midst of a particularly chaotic
era in U. S. history, and the novella (which is set in the late 1960s) incor-
porates the period's dramas into the narrative. It brings the Vietnam
War, racial tension, and recreational drug use into a domestic setting. In
the midst of these conflicts a jaded Italian American screenwriter and
father thinks he would happily trade his bourgeois disappointments for
a *pensione* in Rome and a brunette, "for a change" ("Dog," 11). Of
course, the pull of family proves strong and ultimately overpowers
Henry's fantasies. The overall tone of the novella reflects the story's delicate balance of serious themes and their parodic representations.

When the novella was published in 1986 (along with "The Orgy" in
West of Rome) it received mixed reviews. The *New Yorker* thought it the
weaker of the two novellas, but the *Los Angeles Times* considered "My
Dog Stupid" the "real gem here."[33] The *San Francisco Review of Books* saw

in the novella characteristic Fante traits including "wild humor" and a realistic portrayal of life "at once sensitive and brutal."[34]

On the most basic level, "My Dog Stupid" is a tale of a family in transition. Henry Molise and his wife, Harriet, are watching their children (three sons and a daughter, all in their late teens to mid-20s) leave their Malibu home and start lives of their own. The relationship between husband and wife is very amusing and very familiar: a quiet dinner conflagrates into a fight when one or the other reignites, without warning, a long-standing argument. But the anger expressed in their arguments is balanced by their love life, which remains passionate. The Molise situation might be standard "empty nest" fare except for these mitigating factors: rampant marijuana smoking, making peace with racial miscegenation, the looming Vietnam War draft, and an unmanageable and highly sexed Akita, "Stupid," that takes up residence in the Molise household. Stupid has a kind of cartoonish aggressive homosexuality: he attempts to mount often, and only with male dogs and men. While all these changes are taking place, Henry muses on his life. His career has died, his wife is not as amusing as she once was, and his children, at first glance, are hardly a proud legacy.

The children are, by and large, an unappealing lot. Denny, the actor son, insists on his mother writing his college essays. Harriet does such a good job on a George Bernard Shaw paper that Denny gets an "A" and Harriet gets a letter from the professor congratulating *her* on a job well done. Daughter Tina, still throwing temper tantrums at age 20, uses their house as a home base for her and her surfer boyfriend (just back from Vietnam); they tool up and down the coast in his van, traveling to surf spots and parties, living their own Beach Boys song (leaving father Henry more envious than angry). Eldest son Dominic, the "family's prime screwball" ("Dog," 11), wallpapers his room with pornography and dates only black women, which, as Henry says, "tries his mother sorely" ("Dog," 15). The youngest son, Jamie, is the quiet one, whom his father hardly notices until Jamie is drafted. At that point Henry realizes that his youngest son's innate sweetness and unconditional love is the life lesson Henry has yet to learn.

Jamie is saintly. He secretly quits his job at the supermarket to volunteer at a children's clinic, teaching crafts and sports. His affection for children and animals is beatific, and after the Akita arrives, it is to Jamie's room that the dog goes for the night and in the morning Henry finds them together: "They were both asleep, each on his right side, Jamie's arm around the dog's neck, both snoring. I liked what I saw. I liked boys sleeping with dogs. It was as close to God as they ever got" ("Dog," 33). In the weeks leading up to Jamie's induction into the military, Stupid (whose affection for Jamie alone is strictly platonic) follows the 19-year-old from room to room. Jamie entrusts his father with the good care of Stupid, and Henry promises to abide, though the day after Jamie's induction, a depressed Stupid runs away.

After all the children move out (in fits and starts and amid emotional pyrotechnics) Henry and his wife fill the void with parties. The social events turn into depressing affairs where husbands and wives get potted beyond recognition, television and movie screenwriters take opposite sides in fistfights, and the police must be summoned to break it all up. Soon Harriet develops an interest in pottery and studies the occult, even doing a tarot reading for Henry. Henry's dream to leave everything behind for a simpler life in Italy beckons. More attractive to him than the Italian landscape is the idea of flying away sans Harriet. For her part, the idea of being on her own is not without its appeal.

Henry

Henry imagines being described by someone else, and the image chastens him: "Reputed to be insane, suffering from ulcers, no longer attending Writers' Guild meetings, regularly observed at the liquor store and the State Department of Employment. Or walking the beach with a large, idiotic and dangerous dog. Tedious bore at parties, talking of the good old days . . . Quarreled with agent and currently unrepresented. Talks obsessively of Rome . . . Scorned by his four children . . . Loyal wife tends his personal needs, preparing wholesome meals of custards and soft-boiled eggs, frequently assists him to bathroom" ("Dog," 75). One reviewer read Henry's many complaints as symptomatic of a bad case of Weltschmerz (Crotta, 4).

When the book begins Henry is coming back from meeting a director who wants him to write "a film about the Tate Murders; in 'the manner of Bonnie and Clyde, with wit and style'" ("Dog," 9). Like the repugnant story idea, the financial terms of the job repel Henry. The director offers him no money, but a split of the movie's proceeds. Henry thinks: "It was the third offer of that kind I'd had in six months, a very discouraging sign of the times" ("Dog," 9). Those "times" refer to the film industry in general, as well as Henry's current inability to get an assignment of any kind. His car is three payments past due, and though the house is paid for, it antagonizes him to think that it looks like "what it was not—the domicile of a successful writer" ("Dog," 11). The quality of his fiction is also in a state of decline. When he reads a novel he is 15,000 words into he is shocked to see that it reads like a screenplay: "One chapter began: 'Full Establishing Shot—Apartment House—Day' " ("Dog," 75).

With unpleasant children and a career on the skids, Henry is in grievous need of inspiration and understanding. He remembers fondly his dog Rocco, a bull terrier who, Henry thinks, understood him better than any person ever had, but who was so belligerent that Harriet shudders at the mere articulation of the words "pit bull terrier." When the Akita shows up at his house (wearing a tag that reads: "You'll be sorry") Henry is initially averse to adopting him. Dogs had brought discord to Henry and Harriet's marriage in the past and on the two occasions when Harriet left him, it was over a pet ("Dog," 45).

Henry decides that the dog must stay after a morning when Stupid is attacked by the sovereign dog of the neighborhood, a German shepherd named "Rommel" ("Dog," 39). Stupid fights back and then retaliates by mounting his male adversary (Stupid never manages here or elsewhere to connect, as it were, with any of his victims). Henry admires Stupid's unconventional battle tactics and identifies with the dog since they are both fighters as well as outsiders in this upscale, Anglo-Saxon neighborhood. Henry thinks: "He was a misfit and I was a misfit. I would fight and lose, and he would fight and win. The haughty Great Danes, the proud German shepherds, he would kick the shit out of them all, and fuck them too, and I would have my kicks" ("Dog," 43). Stupid is Henry's perverse doppelgänger, conjured from hell to take his owner's revenge on the world.

That Henry reserves a large portion of his bitterness for his children is understandable: they are, with the exception of Jamie, an aggravating group. But an unreasonable part of his gripe with them is that they are so decidedly Anglo American: "Why weren't they short and stumpy like their father? Why did they resemble store clerks and not stone-masons? Where was the peasant ruggedness of my father and the innocence of my mother, the warm brown Italian eyes? Why didn't they talk with their hands, instead of leaving them hanging dead at their sides during conversations?" ("Dog," 66). He blames his Anglo wife for these Anglo symptoms. He also ruminates on the prejudice he suffered at the hands of her family; Harriet's relatives still refer to Henry as "that Eyetalian boy" ("Dog," 47).

Henry has trouble understanding his children (surely a universal experience). When he tries to rely on the parenting methods his father used—principally violence and ridicule—they seem both outmoded and totally ineffective. In one scene, Henry becomes fed up with Denny's presumptuousness (he thinks his mother *should* write his college essays), and Henry challenges his son to a fight: "Let's go, Buster." Henry walks out the front door and waits, planning to ambush his son: "My plan was to bash him in the mouth as he stepped through the door. I knew he could take me, and all I wanted was that first punch" ("Dog," 31). Henry halfheartedly waits for five minutes, but when the door finally opens it is Harriet telling him that Denny has gone to bed and to please lock all the doors when he comes back inside. His children simply side-step his vitriol, while Henry's own father (assuming it is the Nick Molise of *Brotherhood*) had managed to ensnare his sons in actual combat.

Assuming strong connections exist between this Henry Molise and the Henry Molise of *The Brotherhood of the Grape,* it is safe to call this American offspring the logical manifestation of Henry's journey across the tracks to the "better" side of town. Having worked so hard to escape the world of his Italian stonemason father and to ascend the socio-economic ladder and become an accomplished mainstream writer, Henry now finds himself looking at what he wrought in the process—children assimilated beyond apparent Italian trait. His dream has come to life, but Henry wonders at what cost. Part of his anxiety is clearly connected to his having chosen the American path of assimilation over his Italian peasantry.

The questions raised by the balancing act of assimilation and ethnic tradition (an ongoing theme in Fante novels) is brought to the fore with Katy Dann, Dominic's African American girlfriend. Harriet is outraged at the liaison (and fears the Black Panthers will react violently to Dominic fooling around with "one of their women" ["Dog," 88]). Henry, in his inimitable style, tries to talk to his son about his proclivities for black lovers, and he asks Dominic if he has no sense of "race pride." Dominic lampoons his father's bigotry: " 'Race pride! Say, that's a hell of a phrase, Dad. I'll bet you dreamed it up yourself. It's uncanny. No won-der you're such a great writer.' He crossed to the desk and picked up a pencil and wrote on an envelope. 'Race pride.' I want to write that down so I won't forget it.' " ("Dog," 17). Katy seems to play deliberately on what she knows will be Harriet's stereotype of the highly sexed other by wearing black leather pants and leopard print body suits. The novel highlights, and then ridicules, Henry and Harriet's bigotry. Their chil-dren's impatience and dismissal of their parents' racial prejudice ensures that the miscegenation that Henry and Harriet unreasonably fear will win out. In fact, Dominic and Katy have been secretly married for months. When Henry is given the job of telling his wife about the marriage and also that Katy is pregnant, he first connives to make Harriet smoke marijuana (reasoning that a youth culture drug will soften the shock of youth culture's actions). When Harriet initially balks, Henry feigns outrage: "What a marriage, what a mockery! A man asks to smoke a little pot with his wife, and she chickens out. My God, I'm not asking you to shoot heroin. All I want is for the two of us—man and wife—to join hands in a journey to happyland, where the miseries of life are cast off for a little while" ("Dog," 102–3). Harriet acquiesces.

Henry responds to the changes around him by relying on his strong pride in his Italian background. Unlike any other Fante protagonist, Henry unabashedly longs for Italy. Most of Fante's protagonists are prone to nostalgia and a whiff of Romano cheese can send them into a tailspin of memories of home and their mother's cooking. It is significant that these memories are located in the United States. Henry's nostalgia for Italy, however, is of a different variety: he is homesick for a home that was never his. Further, Henry's father—who is wistfully recalled as a "rugged peasant"—was not even *from* Rome, but the mountainous Abruzzi region. In "My Dog Stupid" Henry's links to his Italian background highlight the synthetic utilization of ethnic tropes. This does not make Italy any less real for Henry, or Henry any less entitled to it, but it is noteworthy for its overt constructedness.

An example of his connection to Italy is shown when Henry prays to the patron saint of Naples, San Gennaro, to deliver him from his American nightmare, soundtrack by Frank Zappa: from Dominic's room came "the mindless rhythms of the Mothers of Invention. I had come to hate the unspeakable illiteracy of that sound, and I lifted my eyes to San Gennaro, and I said to him, how long, O Gennaro, must I suffer?" ("Dog," 14). Henry also prays to San Gennaro to smite his enemies (unpleasant neighbors and a television producer). As noted, his dreams of escape to Rome pepper the novella.

Finally, after Jamie is drafted, Tina married to her surfer, Dominic to the pregnant Katy, and Denny is in New York pursuing acting, Henry decides to sell his belongings and set out for Rome. To raise funds, he sells his car, his tractor, his chainsaw, and his golf clubs, not getting nearly the amount of money he thought he would.[35] He tells the fed up Harriet the reasons for his trip to Rome: "Back to my origins, back to the cradle of civilization, back to the meaning of meaning, the alpha and omega" ("Dog," 133).

After selling his belongings, Henry realizes that he does not really want to go to Rome, but feels that, as a matter of honor (since he made such a production out of it all), he is going to have to go through with the trip. Now having painted himself into a corner he realizes Rome does not sound that appealing at all: "Those cold marble floors sent a chill through my feet. The Romans made bad American coffee. The streets smelled of stale Gorgonzola. . . . I'd miss the World Series" ("Dog," 134). Aside from the discomforts of Rome, Henry is most chilled to think of the reception he would get there as an Italian American writer: "The lowest form of human life was the Italian writer. He walked around with unsold scripts under his arm, his ass showing through thread-bare pants. He despised Italian-Americans, putting them down as cowards who had fled the beautiful national poverty while he, the true patriot, had remained in the fatherland surviving the tragedy of two wars. If you protested that you had no choice in the country of your birth he insulted your father or your grandfather for seeking a better life in another land" ("Dog," 134).

Henry's honor is saved when Stupid, lost for the five weeks since Jamie's military induction, is found. The man who finds the Akita demands a hefty reward and Henry, knowing Harriet will be impressed if he agrees to it, announces his decision to use his Rome funds to get the dog back. Not above playing up his sacrifice, Henry announces: "What's Rome if you have to live with the betrayal of your own son? What's Paris, or New York, or any place in the world? My duty is clear. God knows I have my faults, but I won't stand accused of disloyalty to my children" ("Dog," 135). Harriet (who has shown herself wise enough to see through his charades, no reason to think she cannot see through this one) sighs in admiration at her husband's selflessness. Henry looks into her eyes and sees that they have "bypassed Rome for the moment" ("Dog," 135).

Stupid had made his way to a junkyard in a canyon (it is the junkyard's owner who called him in). When Henry arrives, he sees Stupid happily cavorting with a sweet-natured, smiling pig: "The pig crossed the enclosure to a faucet dripping water into a washtub, Stupid following. She drank and so did he. Then she trotted back to us, staring upward longingly at me, while Stupid licked bits of straw from her sleek back. He admired her tremendously" ("Dog," 138). The junkyard owner offers that Stupid seems to think that the pig is his mother (which fits into Henry's theory of the cause of Stupid's aggressive homosexuality, that the dog was rejected by his mother). Henry learns that the pig is soon to be butchered and while he is negotiating the reward for Stupid, a name pops into his mind: "Mary." It was his mother's name and he thinks of her because she, like the pig, was always smiling. Another $300 later and Henry is driving the station wagon home with an ecstatic Stupid and a smiling Mary.

A corral (left over from Tina's horse phase) is in a far corner of the Molise property, and after he loads Mary and Stupid into the corral, Henry looks around to see vestiges of his children: a basketball hoop, the curtains hanging in the window of his daughter's old room, the remains of a tree house. Surrounded by signs of his children, and overcome by the relief of having chosen home over Rome, Henry begins to cry.

"My Dog Stupid" is very funny, and its tone is often acerbic: characters frequently interact on a harshly sarcastic or simply derisive level. But the novella's ending—which presents Henry at his most sweetly domestic—indicates that the protagonist's bitterness is, finally, overwhelmed by the love he feels for his family. It is a gutsy novella and textbook Fante because he is not afraid to show the flaws in his characters, but not afraid to show their love either.

Chapter Five
Overview of John Fante's Work

When Fante was republished in the early 1980s, readers extolled the author's literary gifts. For instance, in his omnibus review David Thomson ardently maintains that "Fante never wrote a sentence you couldn't sing, or two in a row that don't confuse your urges to laugh and cry. But, as if he was himself so ready to be moved, he made himself write strict and straight, holding the riot in check."[1] Some other critics question Fante's value as a writer: "Black Sparrow Press has done a good deed by reissuing this work. . . . Still, I don't quite see Fante as a writer who had to be resurrected" (Coley, 8). Because Fante *was* resurrected, a critical assessment of his works can only be atypical; we look backward to see how he fits in his own time, and why he evokes such passionate responses now.

Considered by many to be a national treasure, Fante's novels have been judged all the more precious for having been ignored during his lifetime and nearly forgotten altogether. The rediscovery of this previously unknown and unique voice moved Neil Gordon to declare that Fante's "disturbing, singular writing stands alone among American Depression and mid-century writers. He was always the equal, and often the better, of his recognized contemporaries: Fitzgerald, Steinbeck, West, Schulberg" (Gordon, 24). Gordon's comparisons are apt ones, and there is every reason to speculate that before long Fante will commonly be considered better than Schulberg and at least as good as West and Steinbeck.

If Fante's legacy is still in the process of being determined, his appeal is readily apparent; he lyricizes a prevalent version of the very popular American Dream, that of the California Dream. Furthermore, his Southern California is an original. In the genre of Southern California novels, place tends to dissolve onto a palette of itemized grotesqueries, and the region is drawn as absurd and surreal. This stereotype is overt in two seminal Southern California novels: Huxley's *After Many a Summer Dies the Swan* and West's *The Day of the Locust* (both published in 1939, the same year as *Ask the Dust*). Huxley's and West's novels are typical of stories set in Southern California at that time (and today still), which focus on the film industry. Fante was aware of the public interest and commercial potential of a work about the film industry, but he elected to take a more innovative topical direction by writing a novel set in Los Angeles, not Hollywood. *Ask the Dust* originated a Los Angeles that is a lively and complex metropolis. Fante is the first author to pay attention to the details and varied atmospheres of Los Angeles neighborhoods, neighborhoods with distinctions and varieties such as those already recognized from literature set in New York, Chicago, or London. The transience of Los Angeles life is accounted for; all of Fante's characters have a story about how they came to Los Angeles that lends their emigration, sometimes exile, a manifest poignancy. Even in his works that take up the topic of Hollywood, such as *Dreams from Bunker Hill* or "My Dog Stupid," the industry is relegated to the story's outskirts. Fante's works that are set outside Southern California—in both Colorado and the Sacramento Valley—also impress with their settings, but in those novels the landscape feels more like a traditional background. Properties of the landscape recur in these works; Colorado's snow and the Sacramento Valley's sun operate as leitmotifs. The small-town atmosphere of Colorado and the Sacramento Valley contribute to their respective stories, but Fante does not particularize the locales as fully as he does in his urban novels. Fante's small towns are kept in the background; Fante's Los Angeles is front and center.

Another strength of Fante's work is his depiction of the immigrant experience in the West; he focuses on both the Italian patriarch's adjustments to life in the United States and the experience of the second generation, in childhood and adulthood. Fante's characters counter the prejudice they experience by redirecting prejudice outward again. Richard Collins locates the perilous emotional terrain of the immigrant experience and internalized racism displayed by Fante's characters in novels such as *1933 Was a Bad Year* and *Ask the Dust*: "By emulating those now-settled immigrants called Americans, Italian immigrants hoped to assimilate themselves into the alien culture. And yet by adopting the values of the new land, they also adopted the prejudices, perversely calling themselves Dago and Wop with alternating affection and deprecation" (Collins 1991, 44). Attempting to render honestly the compromises made during acculturation, Fante also captures the dynamic processes of ethnic exclusion—where an enthnicity's exchange rate differs by region. The fact that his Italian American protagonists are considered closer to Anglo in Los Angeles than the Mexican American characters emphasizes the arbitrary processes and ironic presence of a palpable social hierarchy in a country that espouses itself an ethnically inclusive melting pot.

One of Fante's best stories was his own life story. The documented creation of an embellished persona began early, in an August 1932 letter to H. L. Mencken, where Fante claimed that he had been born in 1911 "in a macaroni factory which is just the right place for a man of my genealogy to get his first slap, for my people were from the peasantry of Italy . . . My father was very happy at my birth. He was so happy that he got drunk and stayed that way for a week. On and off for the last twenty-one years he has continued to celebrate my coming" (*Correspondence*, 29). It is certainly a good yarn, but he was neither born in a macaroni factory nor was his birth year 1911, but, in fact, 1909. Fante perpetuated this two-year discrepancy in his birthdate, perhaps to give the romantic impression that he was something of a prodigy, a published story writer before his 21st birthday (*Correspondence*, 28).[2]

Often Fante would tempt the margins of verity by claiming that his literature was nonfiction. To an admirer who had asked if the author and his protagonist were the same, Fante unequivocally answered in a 1940 letter: "You want to know if I am Arturo Bandini and I say that I am" (*Letters*, 184). At the end of his life, Fante was asked if the novel he was dictating to his wife (*Dreams from Bunker Hill*) was "autobiographical like the other novels." Fante replied: "Yes. I just help myself to any reminiscences or observations that gathered over the course of my whole life" (Pleasants, 94). Ultimately, though, these works were hardly self-revelatory. Fante did not simply transcribe his life, and, as he later said regarding *Full of Life,* he was just as prone to claim his work was wholly fiction. But unless one is claiming that Fante was a memoirist (and he never did), determining where the truth lies in his work is not relevant. He was at his best when creating fictive worlds in which he was wholly invested.

Fante was, firstly and finally, a deeply personal author. Aside from the stories he published with Filipino heroes,[3] Fante's protagonists are men whose lives very much resemble his own: second-generation Italian Americans who are becoming, or are, writers. Gerald Managan justly observes that in "following the pattern of his own experience so closely, Fante seems not to have displayed any great faculty for pure invention" (Managan, 303). While Managan's critique might be glib, Fante's use of autobiography did sometimes interfere with his literary technique. For example, the Arturo Bandini of *Ask the Dust* rails against his fate in the Anglo-centric landscape and proclaims: "I am poor, and *my name ends with a soft vowel,* and they hate me and my father, and my father's father . . ." (*Dust,* 47; italics added). Here Fante's authorial veil unravels: Fante ends in a soft vowel, not Bandini.

If in a small slip like the aforementioned Fante's own persona overlapped with that of his character's, it should not surprise that Fante was better at articulating the emotions and psyches of his characters than he was at schematizing a strict overall craftsmanship in his novels. Indeed, the formal properties of Fante's work are hardly revolutionary. His plots are straightforward, though they are varied by their episodic shifts. Fante did, however, play with narrative forms in his earlier novels. In *Ask the Dust* Arturo steps out of the first-person point of view that predominates in the novel, to address himself and the reader from a distancing third-person point of view. In *Wait Until Spring, Bandini* the narration is third person, but the narrative focus is split between three characters (Arturo, Mama, and Papa). After these early experiments, Fante's novels are told in the first person and are driven not by complicated plot turns or rhetorical arrangements but by the energy of their characters. The female characters in Fante's novels are rarely as compelling as their male counterparts. Aside from Joyce, the wife in *Full of Life,* and the various incarnations of the mother figure (so important to his meditations on family), the women he created tend to be flat, iconographic characterizations. Fante relied on first-person narration, and on narrators who were like him. That said, it is hardly unexpected that women are usually sidelined in these tales.

Fante was most involved with those characters with which he identified, males whose passions showcase their best and worst selves, and who are forever sabotaging their own desires. Fante's eruptive Bandinis and Molises leave memorable impressions for the author indemnifies them while he so clearly articulates the reasons why they do what they do. Overall, his protagonists are not afforded the luxury of redemption (*Full of Life* is an aberration of this pattern). At the end of *The Road to Los Angeles,* although Arturo Bandini still retains the reader's sympathy, he is actually less likable at novel's end. Over time Fante's characterizations evolved and improved. In *Wait Until Spring, Bandini* (1938) the main characters are generally effusive, and together seem like versions of a prototype. However, in *The Brotherhood of the Grape* (1977) Fante presents a variety of characters; the inclusion of so many more distinctive individuals also contributes to Fante orchestrating more complicated plots and themes.

But even if Fante's handling of themes became more masterful as he matured, these themes never wavered from those he established when he was first published: the experience of the ethnic outsider, of the child in an immigrant family, of the individual grappling with becoming an artist. Novels that Fante wrote later in life, such as *The Brotherhood of the Grape,* basically extended the conflicts inherent in those themes to their adult materializations. Once Fante found his thematic terrain, he did not look much further, and that he did not expand his authorial horizons to other subjects is a criticism that is justly levied at him.

There is something to recommend every novel and novella of John Fante's. I am not alone in considering *Ask the Dust* (1939) Fante's best novel. It is poetic and moving and bravely presents the ethnically diverse world of Arturo Bandini. Not as widely admired, *1933 Was a Bad Year* (1985) deserves more attention for it is an exceptionally well-told story and its characters' struggles with the American Dream are thought provoking. *The Brotherhood of the Grape* (1977) describes, with bracing candor, the tremendous psychological and physical tensions that transpire between parents and children, and over ethnicity and assimilation. "The Orgy" fascinates with its almost fairy-tale sensibilities. "My Dog Stupid" displays Fante at his most sharp and sweet, and also most bitingly humorous.

Perhaps because of the narrow scope of his subject matter, critics have been reluctant to accept John Fante as a major writer. The reason for this must be in part because Fante's works do not correspond with traditional expectations of a great novel. The sustained interior monologues of Arturo Bandini, for example, are more poetic than novelistic; subjects—Los Angeles, love, writing—are transformed from prose to poetry by the vast emotions of the narrator. On the basis of his lyrical prose and the sparking emotions of his psychologically articulate but careening characters, Fante must, without question, be recognized as an outstanding American author. His place sketches ring true. On a more historic level, Fante's depictions of depression-era California and Colorado are invaluable fictional accounts of the complex social and economic negotiations of that time and place. Fante's focus on ethnicity and identity resonate with today's interest in identity politics, and his characters serve to remind us that ethnic identity is a process and fluxes in unpredictable ways.

Neil Gordon regrets that "Fante had not been driven enough, or mad enough, or enough possessed . . . to aim for the place next to Dostoyevsky that should have been his" (Gordon, 29). In spite of whatever promises Fante neglected to keep with fate, Fante carved out a respectable place for himself in American letters. Yes, he had technical and formal limitations. Nevertheless, John Fante is an extremely worthwhile author. On the basis of his many superb novels, John Fante is absolutely entitled to his current critical and popular acclaim; indeed, the attention is long overdue.

Notes and References

Preface

1. An excellent discussion of Fante's short stories is found in the following: David Fine, "John Fante," in *Dictionary of Literary Biography 130: American Short-Story Writers since World War II*, ed. Patrick Meanor (Detroit: Gale, 1993): 156–62; hereafter cited in text.
2. Werner Sollors, "Introduction: The Invention of Ethnicity," in *The Invention of Ethnicity*, ed. Werner Sollors (New York: Oxford University Press, 1989); hereafter cited in text.
3. Thomas J. Ferraro, *Ethnic Passages: Literary Immigrants in Twentieth-Century America* (Chicago: University of Chicago Press, 1993); hereafter cited in text.

Chapter One

1. Ben Pleasants, "The Last Interview of John Fante," *Los Angeles Magazine* 39, no. 2 (February 1994): 90–95; hereafter cited in text.
2. John Fante, *John Fante and H. L. Mencken: A Personal Correspondence, 1930–1952*, ed. Michael Moreau and Joyce Fante (Santa Rosa, Calif.: Black Sparrow Press, 1989), 77; hereafter cited in text as *Correspondence*.
3. John Fante, *John Fante: Selected Letters 1932–1981*, ed. Seamus Cooney (Santa Rosa, Calif.: Black Sparrow Press, 1991); hereafter cited in text as *Letters*.
4. Joyce Fante, interview by author, Malibu, Calif., July 1996; hereafter cited in text as "Interview."
5. Ross Wills, "John Fante," *Common Ground* 1 (Spring 1941): 84–90; hereafter cited in text.
6. The relationship with Helen Purcell must have left a strong impression: Fante wrote of younger men dating older women in *Ask the Dust* and *Dreams from Bunker Hill*.
7. Those stories were "Home Sweet Home" and "First Communion" (collected in *The Wine of Youth*).
8. Mike Davis, *City of Quartz: Excavating the Future in Los Angeles* (New York: Verso Press, 1990).
9. The closeness between the Fantes and the McWilliamses was forever cemented when Carey McWilliams married a high school friend of Joyce Fante's.

10. Mainly an essayist, McWilliams also authored an impressive number of books, most of which centered on California: topics spanned Southern California's history and characters (*Southern California: An Island on the Land* [New York: Duell, Sloan, Pearce, 1946]); working conditions for immigrant labor (*Factories in the Field* [Boston: Little, Brown & Co., 1939]); a history of the Mexican American experience (*North from Mexico* [New York: Greenwood Press, 1948]).

11. The Sleepy Lagoon Murder Trial is often linked to the Zoot Suit Riots and considered part of a campaign against Mexican American youth in Los Angeles. See Gordon DeMarco, *A Short History of Los Angeles* (San Francisco: Lexikos, 1988).

12. Carey McWilliams, introduction to *Southern California: An Island on the Land* (Salt Lake City: Peregrine Smith Books, 1973), xxi; hereafter cited in text.

13. At this time, Maxim Leiber was also the agent of John Steinbeck and F. Scott Fitzgerald.

14. See Jonas Spatz, *Hollywood in Fiction: Some Versions of the American Myth* (The Hague: Mouton, 1969); Leo C. Rosten, *The Movie Colony* (New York: Harcourt, Brace and Co., 1941); Tom Dardis, *Some Time in the Sun* (New York: Charles Scribner's Sons, 1976); Otto Friedrich, *City of Nets: A Portrait of Hollywood in the 1940s* (New York: Perennial Library, 1986); Walter Wells, *Tycoons and Locusts: A Regional Look at Hollywood Fiction of the 1930s* (Carbondale: Southern Illinois University Press, 1973).

15. Fante had applied to go to Italy, and he felt that the biographical piece his friend Ross Wills wrote of him (cited earlier) in Louis Adamic's *Common Ground* cost him the Guggenheim Fellowship. Joyce Fante has written that in the Wills piece "the overall impression is that Fante is something of a clown and not to be taken seriously as a writer. The tone is condescending" (*Letters*, 190).

16. Bruno Domercq, "Grant Him This Waltz," trans. Joyce Fante, unpublished 4-page typescript of an article that originally appeared in French in *Paris Vogue*, November 1989; hereafter cited in text.

17. Another testament to the close friendship between Fante and Saroyan is in the rather odd picture of Fante in a courthouse at Saroyan's divorce hearing; Fante is there as Saroyan's witness (in *Correspondence*).

18. Gerald Managan, "Artist of the Fallen World," in *Times Literary Supplement*, 20 March 1987, 303; hereafter cited in text.

19. Fante's irreverence for matters political is well documented in his letters. In 1936 Fante told McWilliams about a story he wrote called "Communism Comes to Hollywood." He called it a "facetious piece about the millennium and what I shall do when they make me Commissar of filmland" (*Letters*, 135).

20. Though Fante had stories that were up for sale in Hollywood studios at this time, he was not a salaried screenwriter (*Letters*, 150). Joyce Fante supported the couple by working for the Writer's Project, where she contributed to the *W.P.A. Guide to Los Angeles* (Domercq, 1)

21. John Fante, *Dago Red* (New York: Viking Press, 1940).

22. Neil Gordon, "Realization and Recognition: The Art and Life of John Fante," *Boston Review* 28, no. 5 (October/November 1993): 24–29; hereafter cited in text.

23. Fante coauthored one children's book: *Bravo, Burro!* with Rudolph Borchet; illustrated by Marilyn Hirsh (New York: Hawthorn Books, 1970).

24. Frank Spotnitz, "The Hottest Dead Man in Hollywood," *American Film* 14, no. 9 (July/August 1989): 40–44, 54; hereafter cited in text.

25. Fante's artistic interests fused those demonstrated by Towne (1930s Los Angeles in *Chinatown*) and Coppola (Italian Americana in *The Godfather*).

26. Tom Clark, "The Luck of John Fante," *Los Angeles Times Book Review,* 9 April 1989, 14.

27. Charles Bukowski, *Women* (Santa Barbara, Calif.: Black Sparrow Press, 1978).

28. Charles Bukowski, preface to *Ask the Dust,* by John Fante (Santa Barbara, Calif.: Black Sparrow Press, 1980), 5–7.

29. Bunker Hill and Terminal Island, as Fante described them, were long gone by the 1980s. Bunker Hill had gone the way of urban revitalization (discussed at greater length in chapter 3), and Terminal Island had become an industrial landscape after the Japanese internment of World War II removed the fishing population described in *The Road to Los Angeles*.

30. For instance, see Jerry Lazar, "Fante Fever," *California* (April 1989): 122–24. The essay's emphasis on the Fante phenomenon is clear in its subtitle: "Is there anybody in Hollywood NOT making a movie based on a John Fante novel?"

31. David Fine, "Down and Out in Los Angeles: John Fante's *Ask the Dust,*" *The Californians* 9, no. 2 (September/October 1991): 48–51; hereafter cited in text.

32. Alberto Manguel, "Chic Bums," *Saturday Night* 104, no. 3710 (May 1989): 63–65. Dan Fante, John's son, recently wrote a novel—*Chump Change*—that was published (in translation) in France before it found a publisher in the United States. Certainly the French interest in John Fante contributed to that unusual circumstance for his author son. The novel is now available in the United States (*Chump Change* [Northville, Mich.: Sun Dog Press, 1998]).

Chapter Two

1. John Fante, *Wait Until Spring, Bandini* (New York: Stackpole Sons, 1938; Santa Barbara, Calif.: Black Sparrow Press, 1983); hereafter cited in text as *Wait*.

2. John Fante, *1933 Was a Bad Year* (Santa Barbara, Calif.: Black Sparrow Press, 1985); hereafter cited in text as *Year*.

3. John Fante, "The Orgy," in *West of Rome* (Santa Rosa, Calif.: Black Sparrow Press, 1986); hereafter cited in text as "Orgy."

4. Louis Adamic, "Muscular Novel of Immigrant Life," review of *Christ in Concrete,* by Pietro di Donato, *Saturday Review* (26 August 1939): 5.

5. Arturo's age is alternately identified in the novel as 14 and 12. Fante is not the first author to be inattentive to the ages of his characters. In *War and Peace* Leo Tolstoy gives Natasha two different ages (qtd. Robert Hendrickson, *The Literary Life and Other Curiosities* [Orlando, Fla.: Harcourt Brace, 1981], 460.).

6. Fred L Gadarphé, "Left Out: Three Italian-American Writers of the 1930s," in *Radical Revisions: Rereading 1930s Culture,* ed. Bill Mullen and Sherry Lee Linkon (Urbana and Chicago: University of Illinois Press, 1996), 64; hereafter cited in text.

7. Drake De Kay, Review of *Wait Until Spring, Bandini,* by John Fante, *New York Times Book Review,* 23 October 1938, 6–7; hereafter cited in text.

8. This is another strange detail that, like Arturo's vacillating age, seems incongruous and perhaps a mistake on behalf of the author. I tend to think Arturo is 14 and August 12. But it still seems extraordinary that a 12-year-old could grow taller than his 14-year-old brother.

9. Eda Lou Walton, Review of *Wait Until Spring, Bandini,* by John Fante, *Nation* (14 January 1939): 72; hereafter cited in text.

10. Bob Shacochis, "Forgotten Son of the Lost Generation," *Vogue* 177, no. 3269 (December 1987): 190+; hereafter cited in text.

11. Coppola was a fan of Fante's novels and, at different times, had intended to direct versions of *Ask the Dust* and *The Brotherhood of the Grape.*

12. Tom Christie, "Fante's Inferno," *Buzz Magazine* (October 1995): 58–60.

13. Russell Gollard, "An Interview with Joyce Fante and Victoria Fante Cohen," *Stylus* no. 3 (1997): 10–17; hereafter cited in text.

14. Review of *1933 Was a Bad Year, New Yorker,* 2 June 1986, 107.

15. The outbursts of Grandma Bettina—she who sees America as a wasteland—are very similar to those of Donna Toscana of *Wait Until Spring, Bandini.* Donna Toscana is the huge maternal grandmother while Grandma Bettina is the tiny paternal grandmother. Both women are Italian.

16. At this time William Wrigley (of chewing gum fame) owned both the island of Catalina and the Cubs. The Cubs did indeed spend their spring training at Catalina.

17. The chronology of the Molise immigration to the United States is not given in the book. Though Peter's parents live in Roper too, I am assuming that their immigration postdated that of their son.

18. Collins, Richard. "Stealing Home: John Fante and the Moral Dimension of Baseball," *Aethlon* 12, no. 1 (Fall 1994): 81–91; hereafter cited in text.

Chapter Three

1. John Fante, *The Road to Los Angeles* (Santa Barbara, Calif.: Black Sparrow Press, 1985); hereafter cited in text as *Road.*

2. John Fante, *Ask the Dust* (New York: Stackpole Sons, 1939; Santa Barbara, Calif.: Black Sparrow Press, 1980); hereafter cited in text as *Dust*.

3. John Fante, *Dreams from Bunker Hill* (Santa Barbara, Calif.: Black Sparrow Press, 1982); hereafter cited in text as *Dreams*.

4. Will Balliett, "The Undiscovered John Fante," *California* (August 1983): 58, 60; hereafter cited in text.

5. *The Road to Los Angeles* was rejected by a number of publishers, although the rejection letter sent by Stackpole Sons was kind and because of that sensitively worded letter, a new relationship was born: Fante's next two novels would be published by Stackpole Sons (*Letters*, 141).

6. Terminal Island is a real place name. Its rather gloomy name expresses the fact that it marks the terminus of a railway line.

7. When Fante moved to California, he lived with family in the Wilmington area. Later his mother and siblings joined him there. When Nick Fante returned to his wife, the Fantes moved to Roseville, California, and John stayed in the Los Angeles area. After living in Los Angeles and Hollywood, Fante moved back to the harbor area to escape the distractions of Los Angeles and Hollywood and finish work on *Pater Doloroso* (*Letters*, 98). While there, Fante also began work on *The Road to Los Angeles*.

8. Elaine Duffy, "The Great Bandini," *Idler* 21 (January/February 1989): 41–43; hereafter cited in text. Though Duffy does not specify an example of the self-taught ("autodidact") proletarian author, one writer who fits that description is Anzia Yezierska.

9. Edmund M. White, review of *The Road to Los Angeles*, *Los Angeles Times Book Review*, 17 November 1985, 1, 12.

10. "Banning" seems like a tidy Anglicization of "Bandini"; in fact, both Banning and Bandini have historical significance for Southern California. The Bandinis were one of the great Californio families (influential landowners and public figures during the Mexican period). Phineas *Banning*, one of the first Yankee entrepreneurs to displace the Californios when California was ceded to the Union, is considered the founder of Wilmington, California (see Gordon DeMarco). One would have thought that Fante would be deliberate in choosing these appellations, but he was surprised by the significance of Bandini. After *Wait Until Spring, Bandini* was published, the Fantes were contacted by descendants of the Californio Bandinis. Joyce Fante recounted dinners the Fantes shared with the Bandini family, though the relationship did not prove to be a lasting one ("Interview").

11. The crab massacre is horrific. Arturo actually halts his attack on the crabs sunning themselves on rocks to purchase a gun to expedite the annihilation. Fante gives the crabs their revenge in his 1977 novel *The Brotherhood of the Grape*. In that novel, Henry Molise thinks back to his days tramping around the harbor and recalls a particular night spent sleeping on the beach where he is attacked by hundreds of crabs.

12. Stephen Cooper, "John Fante's Eternal City," in *Los Angeles in Fiction*, ed. David Fine, rev. ed. (Albuquerque: University of New Mexico Press, 1995), 83–99; hereafter cited in text.

13. Fante had worked with Filipinos during his pre-Los Angeles time in Southern California. For a long time Fante had intended to write an account of the Filipinos in California in the tradition of John Steinbeck's *The Grapes of Wrath*. *The Road to Los Angeles*'s depictions of cannery work and discrimination show what could have been a kernel of the novel he never finished on the Filipino experience. He abandoned work on *The Little Brown Brothers* in 1944 (*Letters*, 98).

14. In one interlude, Arturo urges a coworker to unionize so that he can make a decent living for himself and his family.

15. As discussed in chapter 2, the protagonist of *1933 Was a Bad Year* contrived to steal and sell a family valuable (a concrete mixer) in an effort to leave home. Richard Collins's essay "Stealing Home: John Fante and the Moral Dimension of Baseball" (in *Aethlon* 12, no. 1 [Fall 1994]: 81–91) discusses the relationship between theft and baseball in Fante's fiction.

16. Wayne Warga, "A Reclamation on Bunker Hill," *Los Angeles Times*, 5 March 1980, View section, pp. 5, 8; hereafter cited in text.

17. E. B. Garside, "John Fante vs. John Selby," supplement to *Atlantic Monthly* 164, no. 6 (December 1939): n.p.; hereafter cited in text.

18. Review of *Ask the Dust*, *New Republic* 101 (6 December 1939): 214; review of *Ask the Dust*, *Saturday Review* 150 (13 January 1940): 80.

19. N.L.R., review of *Ask the Dust*, *Saturday Review* 21, no. 5 (25 November 1939): 20.

20. In the mid-1990s, Angels Flight was taken out of mothballs and made operative; today it is a functioning memoir to a razed neighborhood.

21. Lawrence Clark Powell, *Land of Fiction, Thirty-two Novels and Stories about Southern California from "Ramona" to "The Loved One": A Bibliographical Essay* (Los Angeles: Glen Dawson, 1952); hereafter cited in text.

22. Carey McWilliams, *Southern California Country: An Island on the Land* (New York: Duell, Sloan, Pearce, 1946).

23. Franklin Dickerson Walker, *A Literary History of Southern California* (Los Angeles: University of California Press, 1950).

24. Gerald Volpe, review of *Ask the Dust*, by John Fante, *MELUS* 7, no. 2 (Summer 1980): 93–95. Volpe refers to Camilla and Arturo's relationship as "stillborn."

25. As a point of reference, the Long Beach earthquake took place in 1933.

26. In the Catholic tradition, adultery is any sex outside of the sacrament of marriage.

27. Richard Collins, "Of Wops, Dagos, and Filipinos: John Fante and the Immigrant Experience," *Redneck Review of Literature* 21 (1991): 44–48; hereafter cited in text.

28. Gerald Volpe argues that Vera's death is a kind of self-sacrifice. In a symbolic sense, I think this is convincing. However, since we never know if she really died (she had been out of the apartment when Arturo left it before the earthquake), I think it more accurate that Arturo's imagining her dead makes him less intimidated and therefore confident enough to tell her story.

29. Iris Barry, review of *Ask the Dust,* by John Fante, *New York Herald Tribune Books* 9, no. 9 (12 November 1939): 9; hereafter cited in text.

30. Of course, these are hierarchies that would be consistent with the time and place.

31. Fred L. Gadarphé, *Italian Signs, American Streets: The Evolution of Italian American Narrative* (Durham, N.C.: Duke University Press, 1996), 59.

32. John Fante, *Prologue to Ask the Dust,* with etchings by John Register (Santa Rosa, Calif.: Black Sparrow Press, 1990).

33. Kevin Starr's *Material Dreams: Southern California Through the 1920s* (New York: Oxford University Press, 1990) has a useful chapter that sketches the literary side of Los Angeles and Hollywood that Fante is describing. See "The Book Triumphant: Bibliophilia and Bohemia in Greater Los Angeles."

34. Many of Fante's collected letters testify to his disgust for and distrust of Hollywood (see *Letters* and *Correspondence*). Neil Gordon's essay features interviews with two screenwriters with whom Fante worked. Gordon's essay gives a sense of how Fante was received as a screenwriter and author.

35. The description of Arturo's performance as a busboy echoes that of Camilla Lopez's performance as a waitress in *Ask the Dust.* In *Dreams* Arturo describes himself: "I whirled from table to table, balancing a tray on one hand, and eliciting smiles from my customers" (*Dreams,* 9). In *Ask the Dust* Arturo describes Camilla: "she danced away, swinging the tray gracefully, picking her way through the tables" (*Dust,* 35). Arturo never mentions Camilla in *Dreams,* but that he took up her occupation certainly suggests a connection between the lost Camilla and Arturo and his memories of her.

36. The newspaper photograph of Fante as a busboy is republished in David Fine's 1991 essay.

37. During the composition of this novel, Fante said to interviewer Ben Pleasants: "I just help myself to any reminiscences or observations that gathered over the course of my whole life" (Pleasants, 94).

38. *Nana* tells the story of another fallen woman.

39. Many of Fante's alter egos have relationships with significantly older women. Here Arturo dates Helen Brownell. In *Ask the Dust* Arturo dates Vera Rivken. In *The Brotherhood of the Grape,* Henry Molise has an affair with his father's nurse, another woman who is older, but since Henry is himself 50, the age disparity seems less remarkable.

40. Fante himself was passionate about pinball. His friend, the screenwriter Ross Wills, claimed that Fante's pinball playing actually distracted him from his writing. In his biographical piece, Wills wrote that William Saroyan

(another friend) had modeled the pinball fanatic in his play "Time of Your Life" after Fante.

41. Tony was Tom Mix's horse.

42. See Merry Ovnick's *Los Angeles: The End of the Rainbow* (Los Angeles: Balcony Press, 1994) for a useful discussion of Los Angeles architecture, its motives and expressions.

43. Elaine Kendall, "A Damon Runyon Story Gone West," review of *Dreams from Bunker Hill,* by John Fante, *Los Angeles Times,* 23 March 1982, View section, p. 6; hereafter cited in text.

Chapter Four

1. John Fante, *Full of Life* (Boston: Little, Brown & Co., 1952; Santa Rosa, Calif.: Black Sparrow Press, 1988); hereafter cited in text as *Full.*

2. John Fante, *The Brotherhood of the Grape* (Boston: Houghton Mifflin, 1977; Santa Rosa, Calif.: Black Sparrow Press, 1988); hereafter cited in text as *Brotherhood.*

3. John Fante, "My Dog Stupid," in *West of Rome,* by John Fante (Santa Rosa, Calif.: Black Sparrow Press, 1986); hereafter cited in text as "Dog."

4. In "My Dog Stupid" the protagonist's father's deceased state does not prevent him from retaining a strong presence.

5. The movie starred Judy Holliday and Richard Conte.

6. I will refer to the protagonist as "John" since he is a character in the book, to avoid confusion with "Fante," the author.

7. P. M. Pasinetti, "Immigrants' Children," review of *Full of Life,* by John Fante, *Saturday Review* (26 April 1952): 17–18; hereafter cited in text.

8. Joseph Henry Jackson, "Expectant Father: A Novel," review of *Full of Life,* by John Fante, *San Francisco Chronicle,* 8 May 1952, p. 20; hereafter cited in text.

9. Lem Coley, "California: No Remorse," review of *Full of Life* and *The Brotherhood of the Grape,* by John Fante, *American Book Review* 11, no. 1 (March-April 1989): 8; hereafter cited in text.

10. This is the customary take on how successive generations respond to home nations and the United States and is discussed at greater length in chapter 1. See Rose Basile Green; also, Robert Di Pietro and Edward Ifkovic, eds. *Ethnic Perspectives in American Literature* (New York: Modern Language Association, 1983).

11. Fante featured women prominently in many of his works, but they usually come off as more iconographic than realistic. Camilla Lopez in *Ask the Dust,* for instance, is interestingly contradictory but so distanced as to seem simply a grotesque.

12. Rose Basile Green, *The Italian-American Novel: A Document of the Interaction of Two Cultures* (Rutherford, N.J.: Farleigh Dickinson University Press, 1974), 166.

13. Jane Cobb, "The Fante Family at Home," review of *Full of Life*, by John Fante, *New York Times Book Review*, 15 June 1952, 15.

14. In addition to the very positive reviews of Pasinetti, Jackson, and Cobb cited previously, also see Joe Dever, "Laughter Mixed with Woe," *Commonweal* 56 (16 May 1952): 155–56.

15. One other dated element to the book is that Joyce smokes during her pregnancy.

16. Geoffrey Dunn, "Fante's Paradiso," *San Jose Metro* 7, no. 37 (14–20 November 1991): 15–17.

17. Lionel Rolfe, "John Fante," *California Living* (17 August 1986): 35–36; hereafter cited in text.

18. It should be pointed out that the author of this 1986 article could not benefit from reading works Fante wrote after *Full of Life* that did not find publication until after his death. These include "My Dog Stupid," "The Orgy," and *1933 Was A Bad Year*. When Locklin talks of the slickness of Fante's later works, the critic seems to ignore *The Brotherhood of the Grape*, a later novel that, to my mind, could be decidedly "nast[y] and self-revealing."

19. Brooke K. Horvath, review of *Full of Life*, by John Fante, *Review of Contemporary Fiction* 8, no. 3 (Fall 1988): 169.

20. Michael Mullen, "John Fante," in *Dictionary of Literary Biography: Yearbook 1983*, ed. Mary Bruccoli and Jean Ross (Detroit: Gale, 1984), 103–6.

21. Ben Pleasants, "Stories of Irony from the Hand of John Fante," review of *The Brotherhood of the Grape*, by John Fante, *Los Angeles Times*, 8 July 1979, p. 3.

22. Joe David Bellamy, review of *The Brotherhood of the Grape*, by John Fante, *New York Times Book Review*, 6 March 1977, 30–31.

23. Carolyn See, "Fante Births Another Novel About a Flawed Family," review of *The Brotherhood of the Grape*, by John Fante, *Los Angeles Times*, 3 April 1977, p. 3.

24. Among the topics beyond the scope of this chapter: a very well-written flashback interlude (chapters 8–10) describes a destitute time in Los Angeles for the protagonist (when he was trying to become an author); the relationships between the Molise siblings, whose rivalries and conflicts seem both childish and utterly human.

25. The town is modeled on Roseville, California, the real home of Fante's parents and Joyce Fante's family too. It is called "San Juan" in *Full of Life*.

26. Another story of the conflict of baseball and bricklaying is told in *1933 Was a Bad Year*.

27. Discussed at greater length in chapter 1.

28. The smokehouse is built to smoke meats. Mrs. Ramponi wants to smoke deer meat, specifically. Henry is appalled to hear that she puts corn outside her backdoor and then shoots the deer when they arrive to eat it.

29. Samuel J. Patti, "Recent Italian-American Literature: The Case of John Fante," in *From the Margin: Writing in Italian Americana*, ed. Anthony

Julian Tamburri, Paolo A. Giordano, Fred L. Gadarphé (West Lafayette, Ind.: Purdue University Press, 1991): 329–38; hereafter cited in text.

30. Fante's own experience with diabetes (he had had it for over 20 years when he wrote *Brotherhood*) certainly accounts for the exactitude with which he describes Nick's physical condition.

31. Patti's essay (cited above) does a nice reading of this scene. Patti argues that Fante is emphasizing the passing of the generations by having the brotherhood's final words spoken in Italian.

32. It is significant that a patriarch appears in the book Fante wrote after this one. In *Dreams from Bunker Hill* (1982) the father (dead in *Brotherhood*) appears to Arturo, like a ghost, from out of a snowstorm.

33. Review of *West of Rome*, by John Fante, *New Yorker*, 22 December 1986, 92; Carol A. Crotta, review of *West of Rome*, by John Fante, *Los Angeles Times*, 30 November 1986, Book section, p. 4; hereafter cited in text.

34. Tony D'Arpino, review of *West of Rome*, by John Fante, *San Francisco Review of Books* 11, no. 4 (Spring 1987): 14.

35. The tools and sporting equipment all seem like possessions of the successful American male. Here we see another Fante character who has to sell symbols of the domestic before embarking on a journey away from home. In *The Road to Los Angeles* it was the protagonist's mother's jewelry; in *1933 Was a Bad Year* it was his father's concrete mixer; in "My Dog Stupid" it is the Porsche.

Chapter Five

1. David Thomson, "Los Angeles as Fante's Inferno," *Boston Sunday Globe*, 5 January 1986, Book review section, p. 1.

2. This erroneous birthdate followed him throughout his life. In Rose Basile Green's book on Italian American novelists, Fante's date of birth is given as 1911, not 1909. (*The Italian American Novel: A Document of the Interaction of Two Cultures* [Rutherford, N.J.: Farleigh Dickinson University Press, 1974]). Even in the piece Ross Wills wrote about him for *Common Ground*, the birthdate is given as 1911 (Wills, 86).

3. Fante became interested in Filipinos after living and working with them at the Los Angeles harbor in the early 1930s. His later friendship with Carlos Bulosan may have also contributed to his interest in the Filipino experience. The short stories Fante wrote with Filipino protagonists are "Helen, Thy Beauty Is to Me" (1941) and "The Dreamer" (1947) (both of which are collected in *The Wine of Youth: Selected Stories of John Fante* [Santa Barbara, Calif.: Black Sparrow Press, 1985]), and "Mary Osaka, I Love You," published by *Good Housekeeping* (October 1942). Fante's *The Little Brown Brothers* was the unfortunate name of the novel that he abandoned (it was a known phrase used to describe Filipinos). Fante also considered writing a book about the Mexican beet workers in Colorado, or so he told Richard Donovan of the *San Francisco Chronicle* ("John Fante of Roseville," 9 March 1941, p. 13).

Selected Bibliography

PRIMARY SOURCES

Books

Wait Until Spring, Bandini. New York: Stackpole Sons, 1938; Santa Barbara, Calif.: Black Sparrow Press, 1983.

Ask the Dust. New York: Stackpole Sons, 1939; Santa Barbara, Calif.: Black Sparrow Press, 1980.

Full of Life. Boston: Little, Brown & Co., 1952; Santa Rosa, Calif.: Black Sparrow Press, 1988.

The Brotherhood of the Grape. Boston: Houghton Mifflin, 1977; Santa Rosa, Calif.: Black Sparrow Press, 1988.

Dreams from Bunker Hill. Santa Barbara, Calif.: Black Sparrow Press, 1982.

1933 Was a Bad Year. Santa Barbara, Calif.: Black Sparrow Press, 1985.

The Road to Los Angeles. Santa Barbara, Calif.: Black Sparrow Press, 1985.

West of Rome. Santa Rosa, Calif.: Black Sparrow Press, 1986. Includes the novellas "My Dog Stupid" and "The Orgy."

Prologue to Ask the Dust. Etchings by John Register. Santa Rosa, Calif.: Black Sparrow Press, 1990.

Short Story Collections

Dago Red. New York: Viking Press, 1940. Includes "A Kidnapping in the Family," "Bricklayer in the Snow," "First Communion," "Altar Boy," "Big Leaguer," "My Mother's Goofy Song," "A Wife for Dino Rossi," "The Road to Hell," "One of Us," "The Odyssey of a Wop," "Home, Sweet Home," "The Wrath of God," "Hail Mary."

The Wine of Youth: Selected Stories of John Fante. Santa Barbara, Calif.: Black Sparrow Press, 1985. Reprints the stories in *Dago Red* and also includes "A Nun No More," "My Father's God," "Scoundrel," "In the Spring," "One-Play Oscar," "The Dreamer," "Helen, Thy Beauty Is to Me-."

The Big Hunger: Stories 1932–1959 . Santa Rosa, Calif.: Black Sparrow Press, scheduled for publication in Spring 2000.

Articles

"Bill Saroyan." *Common Ground* 1 (Winter 1941): 75–80.

Screenplays

Dinky (with Frank Fenton). Warner Brothers, 1935.
East of the River (with Ross Wills). Warner Brothers, 1940.
The Golden Fleecing. MGM, 1940.
Youth Runs Wild. RKO, 1944.
My Man and I. MGM, 1952.
Full of Life. Columbia Pictures, 1956.
Jeanne Eagels. Columbia Pictures, 1957.
The Reluctant Saint. Dmytryk-Weiler, 1962.
Walk on the Wild Side (with Edmund Morris). Columbia Pictures, 1962.
My Six Loves. Paramount, 1963.
Maya. MGM, 1966.

Television Plays

Something for a Lonely Man. Universal Television, 1967.

Children's Books

Bravo, Burro! With Rudolph Borchet; illustrated by Marilyn Hirsh. New York:
    Hawthorn Books, 1970.

Interviews

Pleasants, Ben. "The Last Interview of John Fante." *Los Angeles Magazine* 39,
    no. 2 (February 1994): 90–95. Interview conducted near the end of
    John Fante's life by a writer and aficionado well acquainted with Fante
    and his work. In Fante's responses one hears echoes of the bold voices of
    his alter egos. In Fante's recounting stories that would find their way into
    Dreams from Bunker Hill, the reader notes how his written tales and per-
    sonal memories overlap. Only published interview conducted with Fante.

Collected Letters

John Fante and H. L. Mencken: A Personal Correspondence, 1930–1952. Edited by
    Michael Moreau and Joyce Fante. Santa Rosa, Calif.: Black Sparrow
    Press, 1989.
John Fante: Selected Letters 1932–1981. Edited by Seamus Cooney. Santa Rosa,
    Calif.: Black Sparrow Press, 1991.

SECONDARY SOURCES

Bibliographies

Cooper, Stephen. "John Fante's Eternal City." In *Los Angeles in Fiction,* edited by
    David Fine, 83–99. Rev. ed. Albuquerque: University of New Mexico

Press, 1995. The end of Cooper's analysis provides a thorough and briefly annotated update of Mullen's very helpful 1984 working bibliography.

Mullen, Michael. "John Fante: A Working Checklist." *Bulletin of Bibliography* 41, no. 1 (March 1984): 38–41. Bibliography of Fante's works and Fante criticism up to 1984, when interest in Fante was in its early stages.

Articles and Parts of Books

There are many general articles on Fante's life and work that have been printed since 1980; I include a few outstanding examples of those omnibus reviews, but the emphasis here is on essays and chapters that are more analytical.

Bukowski, Charles. Preface to *Ask the Dust,* by John Fante. Santa Barbara, Calif.: Black Sparrow Press, 1980. A heartfelt, three-page tribute to Fante's influence on Bukowski's writing.

Collins, Richard. "Of Wops, Dagos, and Filipinos: John Fante and the Immigrant Experience." *Redneck Review of Literature* 21 (1991): 44–48. The first essay of sophisticated Fante criticism. Insightful close readings of Fante's novels and short stories, focusing on Fante's complex handling of notions of ethnicity.

———. "Stealing Home: John Fante and the Moral Dimension of Baseball." *Aethlon* 12, no. 1 (Fall 1994): 81–91. Shows connections between baseball and Roman Catholicism for Fante's protagonists and showcases *1933 Was a Bad Year,* which, Collins argues, highlights the moral ramifications of the sport of baseball for Dominic Molise. Collins finds in the novel a nexus of baseball, Catholicism, ethnicity, family, and the American Dream.

Cooper, Stephen. "John Fante's Eternal City." In *Los Angeles in Fiction,* edited by David Fine, 83–99. Rev. ed. Albuquerque: University of New Mexico Press, 1995. Argues that Fante's legacy is more profound than simply his regional appeal. Discusses *The Road to Los Angeles, Ask the Dust, Dreams from Bunker Hill.* Reads these novels as puncturing idealized notions of Los Angeles while also "celebrat[ing], even exalt[ing] the rough substance of life as [Arturo] finds it in the rented rooms and sooty streets of old L.A." (84).

Duffy, Elaine. "The Great Bandini." *Idler* 21 (January/February 1989): 41-43. Well-written overview of Fante's works. Compares *Ask the Dust* to Knut Hamsun's *Hunger.*

Fine, David. "Down and Out in Los Angeles: John Fante's *Ask the Dust.*" *The Californians* 9, no. 2 (September/October 1991): 48–51. Discusses *Ask the Dust* in the context of Los Angeles fiction; written by an accomplished scholar of Los Angeles literature.

———. "John Fante." In *Dictionary of Literary Biography 130: American Short-Story Writers Since World War II,* edited by Patrick Meanor, 156–62. Detroit: Gale, 1993. Elegant discussion of Fante's short stories.

Gadarphé, Fred L. *Italian Signs, American Streets: The Evolution of Italian American Narrative* . Durham, N.C.: Duke University Press, 1996. Valuable book of Italian American literary criticism. Includes Fante in chapter called "The Early Mythic Mode," which examines autobiography and autobiographical fiction by Fante and his contemporaries Pietro Di Donato and Jerre Mangione. Discusses the ethnic negotiating Fante's characters perform in light of both literary and historical contexts.

————. "Left Out: Three Italian-American Writers of the 1930s." In *Radical Revisions: Rereading 1930s Culture,* edited by Bill Mullen and Sherry Lee Linkon, 60–77. Urbana and Chicago: University of Illinois Press, 1996. Another version of piece in *Italian Signs, American Streets.*

Gordon, Neil. "Realization and Recognition: The Art and Life of John Fante." *Boston Review* 28, no. 5 (October/November 1993): 24–29. Double query of this impressive essay is: why was Fante not recognized in his own time and why is he receiving so much acclaim today? Most interesting here is Gordon's argument that Fante is best read alongside contexts other than his own: the 1950s of Burroughs or 1920s Paris of American expatriates. Judges Fante to be the equal or superior writer to contemporaries such as F. Scott Fitzgerald, John Steinbeck, Nathanael West, Budd Schulburg. Gordon met with Fante scholars and interviewed two of Fante's fellow screenwriters (Harry Essex and A. I Bezzerides) for this piece and their input on Fante's career and legacy is fascinating.

Green, Rose Basile. *The Italian-American Novel: A Document of the Interaction of Two Cultures.* Rutherford, N.J.: Farleigh Dickinson University Press, 1974. Collection of short scholarly assessments of Italian American authors. Discusses Fante's output in context of his Italian American ethnicity and his position as the son of an Italian immigrant.

Kordich, Catherine J. "John Fante's *Ask the Dust*: A Border Reading." *MELUS* 20, no. 4 (Winter 1995): 17–28. Uses precepts of the border theories of Deleuze and Guattari and others to discuss the myriad ethnic conflicts of *Ask the Dust.*

————. "John Fante's Kaleidoscopic Los Angeles: Roles and Representations of Place in the Arturo Bandini Novels." Master's thesis, San Diego State University, 1994.

Manguel, Alberto. "Chic Bums." *Saturday Night* 104, no. 3710 (May 1989): 63–65. Examines Fante's tremendous popularity among French readers.

Managan, Gerald. "Artist of the Fallen World." *Times Literary Supplement,* 20 March 1987, 303. Wide-ranging, succinct assessment of Fante's oeuvre. Substantively discusses each novel in an even-handed, but overall enthusiastic light. Describes the Arturo Bandini character as "vainglorious" and Fante's protagonists in general as "quixotic."

Matuz, Roger, ed. "John Fante." In *Contemporary Literary Criticism.* Vol. 60. Detroit: Gale Research, 1990. An extremely useful selection of 18 excerpted book reviews of Fante's works from the 1930s to the 1980s.

The time span of these reviews provides an opportunity to see how Fante was seen by critics of different generations, particularly since Fante's 1930s novels were republished in the 1980s. The most apparent difference noted in these reviews is that characters described as "typically Italian" in the 1930s are deemed "stereotypically Italian" in the 1980s.

Patti, Samuel J. "Recent Italian-American Literature: the Case of John Fante." In *From the Margin: Writing in Italian Americana,* edited by Anthony Julian Tamburri, Paolo A. Giordano, and Fred L. Gadarphé, 329–38. West Lafayette, Ind.: Purdue University Press, 1991. Charts trends in Italian American narrative by using the specific examples of Fante's *Wait Until Spring, Bandini* (1938) and *The Brotherhood of the Grape* (1977).

Shacochis, Bob. "Forgotten Son of the Lost Generation." *Vogue* 177, no. 3269 (December 1987): 190, 192, 202, 210. One of the best omnibus reviews for its analysis and narrative spark. Puts Fante in context with his literary brethren.

Spotnitz, Frank. "The Hottest Dead Man in Hollywood." *American Film* 14, no. 9 (July/August 1989): 40–44, 54. Assesses Hollywood's response to Fante's novels and accounts for the option frenzy for Fante's novels during the late 1980s. Spotnitz has gone on to film a documentary of Fante's life. To date, it is still in production.

Wills, Ross B. "John Fante." *Common Ground* 1 (Spring 1941): 84–90. A colorful, anecdotal character sketch of John Fante by one of his closest screenwriter friends. Fante was not pleased with the piece and believed that it made him appear clownish and ultimately cost him the Guggenheim Fellowship for which he had applied.

Index

The Author

Catherine J. Kordich is a Ph.D. candidate in literature at the University of California, Santa Cruz. She has authored essays on John Fante and San Diego's Panama California Exposition of 1915 and published interviews with poet Janet Lewis and opera composer Alva Henderson.

The Editor

Joseph M. Flora earned his B.A. (1956), M.A. (1957), and Ph.D. (1962) in English at the University of Michigan. In 1962 he joined the faculty of the University of North Carolina, where he is professor of English. His study *Hemingway's Nick Adams* (1984) won the Mayflower Award. He is also author of *Vardis Fisher* (1962), *William Ernest Henley* (1970), *Frederick Manfred* (1974), and *Ernest Hemingway: A Study of the Short Fiction* (1989). He is editor of *The English Short Story* (1985) and coeditor of *Southern Writers: A Biographical Dictionary* (1970), *Fifty Southern Writers before 1900* (1987), and *Fifty Southern Writers after 1900* (1987). He serves on the editorial boards of *Studies in Short Fiction* and *Southern Literary Journal*.

LSTR